The Power of Healthy Tension

Overcome Chronic Issues and Conflicting Values

Unite Your Team. Spark Change. Get Unstuck.

Tim Arnold

HRD Press, Inc. • Amherst • Massachusetts

Published by: HRD Press, Inc.
                 22 Amherst Road
                 Amherst, Massachusetts 01002
                 1-800-822-2801 (U.S. and Canada)
                 (413) 253-3488
                 (413) 253-3490 (fax)
                 http://www.hrdpress.com

ISBN 9781-1-61014-414-8

Get ready to tap into
The Power of Healthy Tension

I meet with leaders all the time who are passionate, talented, and innovative but who are still struggling to get their teams to perform at the level they know is possible. Most leaders don't know that the thing they're most *avoiding*—tension—is the very thing that could explode the growth and effectiveness of their team.

In this book, I can show you how to:

- **Unite your team:** Give your team the shared language they need to move from conflict to collaboration, where everyone is heard and understood.

- **Spark Change:** Find out why it is hard for people to shift their thinking, and learn the skills to promote healthy change that your team will support.

- **Get Unstuck:** Break through chronic issues and conflicting values to regain effectiveness, energy and enjoyment.

Want to see how well your organization is tapping into the power of healthy tension? Take the quiz:

www.thepowerofhealthytension.com/quiz

Praise for The Power of Healthy Tension

Tim has done an excellent job of bringing to life the power of first recognizing, and then learning to use, the power of apparently competing realities when dealing with life's challenges. He clearly illustrates his explanations with many examples drawn from personal experience that provide the reader with real clarity. The book is also well augmented with opportunities for personal reflection and application, the interactive nature of which make it practical, relevant, and well worthwhile food for thought.

Phil Geldart, CEO
Eagles Flight

The Power of Healthy Tension will stimulate your heart and mind. Working in a world of polar opposites—poverty and affluence—I used to view all of our organization's chronic issues as problems to be solved. I now have realized that many of these situations are instead tensions to be managed. This book has equipped me with practical tools and down-to-earth applications that make sense of the complexities in life. Read it as a sacred script.

Dr. Barry Slauenwhite, Present and CEO
Compassion Canada

The complexity involved in operating a city is significant. Tim has created an easy to understand and effective way to understand the necessities of healthy tension in decision making—and in life. Through an understanding of polarities, and the need to find balance between conflicting values, Tim has created a valuable guide for people looking to lead a more focused and balanced life.

Walter Sendzik, Mayor
City of St. Catharines

As a Senior Leader within the Addictions and Mental Health world, this book is a must read. The complexity that we must navigate as a result of sweeping restructuring in the healthcare system can be overwhelming, and this book is like a complexity fitness coach. The relevancy of the stories that are so well articulated bring our tensions to life. A masterful book that will coach you as you exercise the power of healthy tension.

Garry Laws, CEO
Addictions and Mental Health Services
Hastings Prince Edward

After Tim Arnold taught our team about Healthy Tension, I have never faced a problem quite the same way. It felt like a veil of uncertainty and frustration had lifted off every weary problem and frustrating circumstance. Great challenges, the type that seemed unresolved, now snapped into focus.

John T. McAuley, President and CEO
Muskoka Woods
Author, *Leading from In-Between*

Life can be full of problems, but it seems that it's the tensions to manage that are the toughest challenges. Tim has taken some very technical concepts and made them user-friendly for our everyday— at work, in our homes, and with our friends and families.

Jeff Lockyer, Lead Pastor
Southridge Community Church

Polarity management is an excellent tool to surface solutions in those frequent situations where driving for a yes/no answer isn't the right approach, but the mechanics of the tool can seem clinical and hard to apply in real life. Tim's stories clearly show the human side of polarity management and how to use it to create positive outcomes for the non-binary issues we deal with every day.

Mary Turner, Retired President and CEO
Canadian Tire Bank

Hardly anybody truly enjoys living in tension, but we all do it out of necessity. The concepts of polarity management that Tim Arnold so cogently articulates address the instincts that cause most of us to respond to tensions with avoidance or conflict. Many readers of this fine and immensely practical little book will slap their foreheads and say, "Of course!" Tim explains a great deal that most of us half know already, but don't have enough clarity to put into consistent practice. Whether it's a matter of parenting, personal or work relationships, I guarantee you'll find this book tremendously helpful.

Greg Paul, Author: *God In the Alley*
Sanctuary Toronto

Tim Arnold has written an incredibly helpful and clear account of the deep wisdom that comes with managing polarity and cultivating healthy tension. The inspiring examples Tim uses employ the strategy he outlines and encourage the reader to integrate this strategy in all areas of life. As a practitioner committed to cultivating both safe and diverse community, I am grateful that Tim has written such an accessible and understandable book and hope it will be widely read and applied.

Dr. Wendy VanderWal Gritter, Executive Director
Generous Space Ministries

Bravo! Great dissection and explanation of Polarity Management and the Power of Healthy Tensions. I don't believe in coincidences; reading this book came during a time in my leadership journey that has assisted me in understanding and overcoming tensions to deliver a principle value.

Brian Hutchings, Vice President, Administration
Brock University

What makes this book so exceptional is that you will be learning from a master teacher who invites you into his world of leadership in a vulnerable and authentic way in order to bring every principle of Polarity Management alive. He shares examples, both common and riveting, that help the reader understand. It is a compelling case why healthy tension is essential for all leaders regardless of their personal or professional background. Be prepared to learn and be inspired.

Bonnie Wesorick, RN, MSN, DPNAP, FAAN
Founder/CPM Resource Center

About 10 years ago I attended a workshop conducted by Tim Arnold on the topic of Polarity Management. It truly changed my life forever. I now see my different roles, like that of a social work practitioner, a husband, a father, and a person of faith, through the lens of managing polarities within the core values inherent in these roles. Tim's book, *The Power of Healthy Tension*, beautifully introduces the concept of Polarity Management and outlines its application in both one's personal as well as professional life. I'd highly recommend it to anyone.

Dion Oxford, Mission Strategist
The Salvation Army, Housing and Homeless Supports

Tim Arnold writes the same way he lives—thoughtfully processing life from the sacred middle ground of a very bright mind and a very deep heart. It is then no surprise that Tim's uniquely insightful book drives readers to a place that neither bends too far into sheer intellect or bows too far into gooey sentiment, but rather finds that sweet spot of balance that truly nurtures the notion of "thriving". All of this adds up to an important read for people who dwell in any societal orbit—from social-justice to high finance, home-making to empire building, street smart to book smart—as a means to explore, understand, embrace and flourish through life's inevitable tensions.

Tim Huff, Award-winning, Best-selling Author/Illustrator
of books for adults and children,
Creative Lead for "The Compassion Series"—
a program of Youth Unlimited (YFC)

Tim Arnold isn't messing around with *The Power of Healthy Tension.* He takes systems thinking to a much-needed place by making it accessible and engaging for our everyday life. He gives the reader a real gift by bringing together his vast experience, personal stories, authentic perspective, and down-to-earth writing style; one can't read *The Power of Healthy Tension* without feeling compelled and equipped to approach problems differently. I've personally been impacted by Tim's book and I've seen first-hand the positive impact it has on emerging leaders of the next generation.

Christa Hesselink, Director
Next Generation Engagement, BIC Canada

Dedication

This book is dedicated to Dr. Barry Johnson—a role model, a mentor, and a wonderful friend. His work is making our world a better place by enhancing the way we think, and his friendship is making me a better person.

Table of Contents

Foreword

What if the tensions in our lives could become a powerful resource to support our dreams rather than a source of endless nightmares? This is a real possibility with the perspective Tim is bringing to us in this book. It could be a tension we experience with another family member over a political issue. At a larger level of system, it could be the tensions built in to addressing differences and privilege within gender, race, class, or religion. When we experience these tensions, a very important question to ask is whether the tension is essentially a problem to solve or a polarity to leverage. If it is a polarity to leverage, it will be unavoidable, unsolvable, and unstoppable.

The natural tension within the polarity, if treated as a problem to solve, could easily become an endless nightmare. Yet Tim helps us convert this natural tension into a resource for building relationships rather than destroying them; for seeing our "enemy" more completely and loving them; for moving polarization to optimization. This book is for those who experience some tensions in your life and would like these tensions to work for you and the community rather than against you and the community. It is for those who care about the needless suffering in our world and want to do something about it beyond blaming the "other". This book is for you.

Tim Arnold and I have been on a learning journey together for several years. During that time, I have witnessed his wonderful combination of humility *and* self-assurance; of curiosity *and* compassion; and his ability to introduce polarity thinking to people from all walks of life. He is equally at ease with chief executives and the homeless. He lives polarity thinking rather than just talking about it as a useful concept. He breathes it into his being a husband, a parent, a leader, a coach, and a friend. No matter your position in life, Tim speaks to you in plain language about enhancing your life and making a difference in the many settings in which you find yourself.

Barry Johnson, author of *Polarity Management*
and originator of the Polarity Map®

Introduction

Tension as Your Greatest Asset

When I was growing up, tension was generally viewed as a negative thing. In fact, for me, tension was something to be avoided at all costs. Honestly, I think this is true for most people. I've spent the past two decades working with teams and the common thread I've seen everywhere is that people are terrified of conflict, avoiding it, even tiptoeing around the issues they know carry the most tension.

If only they knew tension could be their greatest asset and ally.

I've come to realize that there is a certain kind of tension that can be incredibly positive. A form of tension that I am learning to embrace—*healthy tension*.

As humans, we tend to naturally see things from a right or wrong, good or bad perspective, and take an either/or approach. However, research shows there is *another* way to approach life that is incredibly powerful. In fact, this can bring new vitality to your business partnerships, passion to your teams, it can re-route old bad habits and even save failing businesses and organizations. In this book, I'll share with you some of the incredible insights I've gained as to what it takes to be able to embrace a both/and perspective and tap into the power of healthy tension.

Let me tell you how my adventure with healthy tension started...

When I was finishing my undergraduate degree, I had a pretty good hunch that I wasn't going to pursue a job where I would use my training in accounting in a typical way. I spent a few years being a corporate facilitator, and then for a decade I owned and operated my own consulting company focused on team-building and leadership development. This gave me the privilege of working with hundreds of organizations ranging from Fortune 500 companies to The United Nations.

And then, about 10 years ago, I sold my company and embarked on a totally new career path.

At that time, the church I attended wanted to be more involved in local outreach and to have a real, long-term impact on those in need in the community around us. This was something I was greatly interested in being part of. To be honest, though, none of us had any idea where to start, so we began having a lot of conversations. We talked with the mayor, with the regional council, with a number of social service professionals, essentially saying, "Hey world, we've got space and a lot of volunteers and we're open to anything." That resulted in the mayor and the city council asking if we would consider sheltering the homeless.

We agreed, and less than two weeks later 60 people from the street slept in our church building and we have never closed our doors since—taking in more than 8,000 homeless people and serving close to 450,000 meals. Two years into the shelter's existence, I moved from my volunteer role into a staff position, and started directing the shelter full-time.

I tell you all of this for a few reasons. One is so you will understand why some of the examples I use throughout this book are taken from my consulting experiences, and others come from my *day-job*, featuring the people we are reaching out to in the margins of society.

Another reason is to show you how strongly I believe in and rely on the content of this book. I thought, when I sold my consulting company, that I was leaving behind all the theories and business models that I taught on a weekly basis. Instead, I have come to realize that my consulting work was just the training ground for my current role, a role in which I find myself living out this idea of healthy tension every single day.

All of that to say, this book won't just help you to become a better business leader... it's a powerful way to bring peace and hope to our hurting world.

I've also learned that it is *way* easier to *talk the talk* about holding things in tension than it is to *walk the walk*. I often struggle! However, even though it is challenging, I believe now more than ever that tapping into the power of healthy tension is a foundational and non-negotiable skill for any person, leader, or team trying to make the world a better place.

That is what this book is about—it is a guide to help you understand how to embrace healthy tensions in your workplace, your family, and your relationships. I trust that it will help you thrive in all the adventures life has in store for you.

The Long Precedent for This Way of Thinking

The phenomenon of healthy tension, polarities, and paradox has been around forever, and as a result countless people have talked about, studied, and written about it. This has resulted in powerful teaching throughout the ages, including Lao Tzu's exploration of yin and yang, Jesus Christ's teaching on grace and law, and Jim Collins' findings around "the genius of the AND".

As you will grasp from the book's dedication, my understanding of healthy tension comes from my training in a model developed by Dr. Barry Johnson called *Polarity Thinking*™. The ideas in this book are based on this model and theory. I want to share with you how this way of thinking, communicating, and decision-making has proven powerful for me as a leader and in the work I do on a daily basis. I hope this book explains complicated ideas in language that is easy to understand and use—so that you can start to implement these tools in small ways, for big results, right away. These ideas have become an important part of my personal (and my team's) vocabulary every day—and I am confident that they will be useful for you too. I am deeply honored that Dr. Johnson and the Polarity community have given me their blessing to offer my perspective on these concepts, and am forever indebted to them for all of their work that has allowed me to get to this point.

Ready for a Change?

I know you believe in the work you're doing and want to be successful. At the same time, my guess is you're struggling. You're a bit stuck. You know there is greater capacity for you and for your team than you've seen actualized yet. I imagine you lay awake at night and wake up every morning, trying to innovate and adjust the way you're doing things to see greater results. Consider this your warning that everything is about to change. The concepts I will present to you in this book are so powerful, when you implement them, you'll see results immediately.

- Live out your mission, vision and values
- Resolve chronic organizational issues
- Turn your least productive team members into your *most* productive team members by shifting their mindsets
- Implement change without the typical backlash
- Engage in difficult conversations and leverage them to your advantage

When you truly grasp the phenomenon of healthy tension, it changes everything. You will never look at your work, your home, or your relationships the same way.

You won't be able to, even if you try.

I say this—and write this book—with great excitement. As we see and understand key tensions in our lives, we are able to embrace them and leverage them over time. This literally has the power to change our world. It gives us a greater ability to love and accept ourselves and those around us, even those we often view as unlovable or detestable. It gives us a greater ability to resolve and minimize conflict while learning to enjoy healthy opposition. It gives each of us a greater ability to be a person who promotes and embodies peace, harmony, and joy.

However, all of this comes at a cost: ongoing hard work. Once we choose to tackle conflicting values head on and embrace their tension, it is like trading in a recreational paddleboat for a white-water kayak—replacing relaxation with non-stop, in-your-face adventure.

So, I warn you—this is not for the faint of heart. Sizing up the conflicting values that you face and striving to achieve healthy tension is one of the most challenging things you can do in life. Unless you approach your work, your home life, and your relationships with an "all-in" mentality, you will be better off closing this book right now.

However, if you are up for the challenge and want to see your work, your home, and your relationships thrive—no matter what the cost—then keep reading. I promise you, it will be worth it.

SECTION ONE

The Basics

Big Waves and Rip Tides ━━━

In life, we are constantly facing two types of challenges: **problems to solve** and **tensions to manage**. Getting the two confused or not knowing the difference can be deadly—to our work, our leadership, and our relationships. However, knowing the difference and dealing with each type of challenge appropriately will allow us to thrive. Let me explain.

Ten years after university graduation, my dormmates reunited in Carlsbad, California for a week of surf school. We were told—guaranteed!—that by the end of the week, we'd all be surfing. Based on this guarantee, I had a picture in mind of how this would look: I'd be standing confidently on my surfboard, conquering 10-foot waves that curled over my head. The real picture of how my surfing looked at the end of the week was quite different (and a little bit embarrassing), but I had a ton of fun and left with a lot of new knowledge.

Probably the most interesting thing I learned was just how the ocean works. On our first day of surf school, our instructor had us stand on the beach and stare at the incoming waves. He said, "Everyone thinks they know how the ocean works—that the waves are out there and they come into the shore, so we just need to paddle out and ride the waves to the beach." But then he said, "Have you ever thought about where that water goes? When all these waves come in, where does the water go to—how does it get back out to the ocean?" Although I had been born and raised near the Great Lakes, I realized that I had very little ocean insight and was quite interested in where he was going with the conversation. He then explained to us how it worked. Yes, all the water comes to shore through the waves, but then this water eddies along the shore, forming what is like a river that flows perpendicular to the shore, taking the water back out into the ocean. This river is called a rip tide or a rip current. Rip tides are not easily visible unless you are looking for them, but if you stand on the shore you can identify them and see them in action.

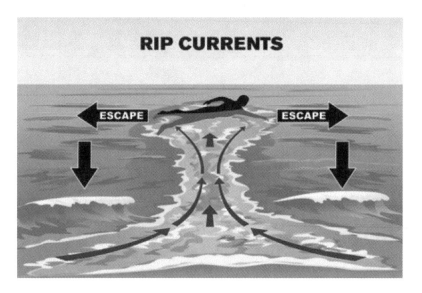

And it wasn't just interesting trivia, either. Our instructor said that people come to surf school assuming that the greatest danger in the water is sharks, but what they don't realize is that the real danger is in how you respond to rip tides. These unexpected currents take people by surprise, and at times end up taking lives.

Getting caught in a rip tide happened to me. I was paddling out on my surf board, trying to get out to some good waves, when I suddenly looked up and realized that I was out *way* farther from shore than I expected (or wanted) to be. I had been carried out by a rip tide. What the instructor had said was true: everything in my gut desperately wanted to swim toward shore as hard as I could. It was all I could do to fight this instinct.

That is why my instructor started the week out by teaching us about rip tides, because if you go with your gut and just swim toward shore, you can die. You cannot swim against a rip tide because it is too strong. Despite your intention and hard work, you will end up drifting farther and farther away from where you want to be. Eventually you will get exhausted and drown. Instead, you have to go against your natural instinct to swim for shore and turn and swim parallel to shore just for a while, and all of a sudden you will find yourself out of the rip tide. You can then ride the waves safely back into shore.

When I found myself drifting out deep into the ocean, it took everything I had to fight my drive to swim to shore and, instead, force myself to deliberately turn. But I did this and started swimming parallel to shore and within no time, I realized that I was out of the dangerous current and that the waves were helping me get back to shore. It was an experience I will never forget.

What was fascinating to me had to do with the real surfers—the good ones like those in the picture on page 9. The first thing they do when they arrive at the beach is take some time to study the shoreline and look for the riptides. They do this because they know that riding these currents out to the big waves will save them a ton of time and energy. In the same time that it took for me to splash and flail my way out to one good wave, by leveraging the riptides these real surfers had often ridden five or six of them. They take something that can hurt somebody, and instead of fearing it, they embrace it and leverage its unique power for their fun and advantage.

I tell you this story because I think it is a great metaphor for what you are about to read. In our lives, our relationships, and our work, it's easy to size up every challenge that we face as a **problem to solve**, and to take a right or wrong, good or bad, either/or approach. Often, we are correct in using this approach because we are faced with lots of problems to solve each and every day. They are like the non-stop waves that come into the shore.

But sometimes we encounter a different kind of situation in our lives, a **tension to manage,** in which traditional problem solving will no longer work for us. It's similar to a riptide, where if we treat this type of situation with the conventional wisdom of problem solving, the harder we try, the further away we find ourselves from the exact place we want to go. I have seen this divide teams; I have seen it derail leaders; I have seen it devastate families; and I have seen it blow up organizations.

Yet when you look at really effective leaders and organizations that are thriving, they are much like the pro surfers. They understand and hold onto the wisdom of problem solving, using this either/or approach when it serves them well. However, they also realize that problem solving is not enough—that there is another undercurrent at play at work and in life; situations that require them to hold conflicting values in tension with a both/and approach. They embrace situations that others find exhausting and dangerous, and leverage the energy to their advantage. When you see these people, they stand out. These are the kind of people who have the ability to change the world in a positive and powerful way. They have tapped into the power of healthy tension.

Healthy Tension

Let's start with what *we are not* going to focus on too much in this book: problem solving. A situation is a problem to be solved when there is a) one right answer, or b) two or more right answers, but you can still choose only one option and solve the problem completely. I am thinking of things like policies, procedures, formulas, history, and situations where there is a superior alternative. Problem solving requires an either/or approach, meaning that you choose *either* one answer *or* the other.

Effective problem solving is critical for survival at work and at home. I want to be absolutely clear that in my enthusiasm for healthy tension, I am not belittling, undermining, or rejecting problem solving and either/or thinking.

There are two reasons we are not going to focus much on problem solving. The first reason is that you do not need my help. We develop our problem-solving skills very early in life, and are continually respected and rewarded for solving problems well, so you are probably already quite good at it.

The second reason is that our society already has a bit of an obsession with problem solving.

Problem solving dominates our approach to education, religion, and politics, which makes it easy for us to see *everything* as either/or, good or bad, and wrong or right. My hope is that this book offers a new perspective, an approach that supplements your ability to solve problems, and as a result, allows you to thrive in a new way at work and at home. This fresh approach allows you to embrace conflicting values and harmonize diverse points of view. It is called Healthy Tension.

The good news is that while the expression Healthy Tension might be new to you, in reality it is something you have been engaged in your entire life. What we are going to do throughout the book is take some time to make it a bit more conscious and much more deliberate.

The bad news is that because of society's obsession with problem solving, we often treat every challenge we face as a problem to solve, and end up frustrated, confused and overwhelmed. Let me show you what this looks like.

My Parenting Dilemma

A few years ago, when my wife Becky was expecting our first child, we realized that since both of us had been the baby in our families, neither of us had ever really had much experience with kids. We felt really ill-equipped for this huge responsibility of raising children of our own.

People often give expectant parents advice—whether they want it or not. In our case, we wanted it! And in the months that followed the announcement that we were expecting, we were completely blown away by the amount of unsolicited parenting advice people gave us. People offered us books and referred us to websites and YouTube videos they said we had to check out. They told us personal stories from their experiences. They handed us medical research. They gave us everything we needed to become great parents. And we were like sponges, soaking it all in.

But eventually it started to be not so fun, because we realized we were faced with a dilemma and were going to have to make a decision.

EFFECTIVE PARENTING

Flexibility   vs.   Structure

You see, there seemed to be two camps of parenting. On one hand, there were people handing us books, stories and statistics who believed that effective parenting comes down to **structure**. They talked about the Ferber Sleep Method and how ultimately, the consistency and routines you put in place from day one are what dictate how well-adjusted your child is as a toddler, child, and even young adult. We listened and said, okay, we can do that. **Structure** it is!

This parenting "solution" felt great until we talked to the next person, who was in the other camp, the one that says that the most current research shows that effective parenting really comes down to **flexibility**. These parents talked about *attachment parenting* and how our #1 job is to figure out what we can do to flex our lifestyle around our child's needs, and to be as responsive and attached to the child as possible—especially in the first few months. They, too, would back up their ideas with research, books, medical opinions, and testimonials.

Around the six-month marker in the pregnancy, we were pretty much done with unsolicited advice. It was no longer encouraging. We did not know what side to choose. It had also become clear that Becky and I had different points of view, which made the situation all the more frustrating.

We ultimately decided that we would stop reading the books, would ignore the websites, and would even learn how to politely decline unsolicited advice. Instead, for the next three months, we would try to identify some parents we really admired and hang out with them as much as possible. They would be our teachers!

We each made an independent "awesome parents" list, compared them, exercised a few vetoes, had a few arguments, and finally came up with three sets of people whose parenting we admired. Then we decided to invite them all over for dinner the next weekend.

At first, when they arrived it was somewhat awkward. They didn't all know each other and we had not told them about our plan for the evening. But we quickly introduced them, explained our dilemma, and told them we had specifically invited them because we liked what we saw in their parenting and we wanted to learn from them. We asked that for the rest of the night, they would simply share their best-case scenario parenting stories, times when they felt like somehow, they were doing it right—whether for a moment, a day, or a season.

After a slow start (and a bit of wine), the stories came fast and furious, and we talked until one o'clock in the morning. What was fascinating to me, though, was that when the last car drove away and Becky and I spent hours debriefing the experience, we realized that in the countless stories we had heard, no one had mentioned a specific theory or model. No one said we had to read this book or that study. All the stories were completely unique—yet every couple generally said the same thing: "We've been our best as parents when on the one hand we're incredibly **structured**—having lots of routine and consistency. And at the same time, we do this in a totally **flexible**, day-by-day way." (And then they would add that when you've got it all figured out, the "solution" rarely works with the next kid!)

On the one hand, we were a bit discouraged because we did not get the perfect theory or list of "seven steps to effective parenting" that we had hoped for, but at the same time, we felt like we had had a bit of an epiphany.

We realized that effective parenting was not going to be a problem that we solved with an either/or approach. Instead, it would require a both/and mindset. Parents were at their best when they were able to embrace *both* **structure** *and* **flexibility** over time. This dilemma was not a problem that we could ever solve. Instead, it was a tension that we needed to accept and embrace. The more comfortable we became with the dance of **structure** and **flexibility**, the more we would move toward our ultimate goal (or Higher Purpose) of being **effective parents.**

EFFECTIVE PARENTING

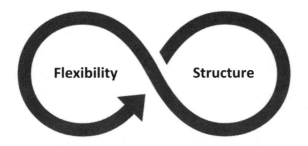

This isn't just true for parenting. In our lives—both at work and at home—we are constantly facing situations similar to flexibility vs. structure. Situations where there will be no *one* solution, no fix, no perfect way. For the remainder of this book, I will refer to these conflicting values, such as flexibility vs. structure, as ***polarities***. Our goal is to be able to identify the important polarities in our lives; for example, Work vs. Home or Planning vs. Action, and ensure that we are achieving *healthy tension* between the conflicting values.

Polarity:

- A situation in which two ideas, opinions, etc., are completely opposite from each other, yet equally valid and true.

- A situation in which two opposing ideas exist in seemingly impossible tension.

COMMON POLARITIES

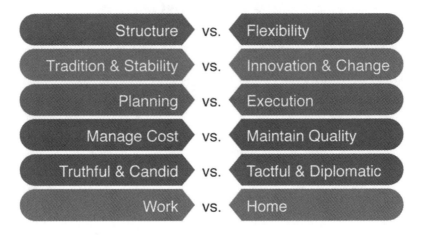

The good news is that we can learn the type of thinking that helps us manage these polarities in a healthy way. Jim Collins, author of *Good to Great*, explained this by using the term, "The Genius of the AND". My mentor and friend, Dr. Barry Johnson, refers to this as Polarity Thinking™. Throughout this book, I will refer to it simply as *healthy tension*. Let me show you what I mean using a simple but powerful metaphor: breathing.

Just Breathe!

It is interesting: we breathe about 25,000 times a day and, for the most part, we do not even think about it. Breathing is one of the automatic processes in our body, like digestion. It just happens, even when we are asleep. And yet if our natural breathing pattern is off or disturbed, we quickly end up in trouble.

When I was in university, I had a part time job as a rock-climbing instructor. When I was being trained as a guide, I learned that when someone is climbing, it is very common for them to hit what we referred to as the "freak-out zone". A person might only be a foot off the ground or they might be a hundred feet up the climbing wall, but all of a sudden fear gets the best of them and they cannot go up and they cannot come down. They are frozen in a kind of trance.

What is interesting is that when someone is in the freak-out zone, it is useless to give them more climbing instruction or a motivational speech. The best thing to do is to have them look you in the eye and tell them to simply breathe. Just breathe. For whatever reason, they have lost touch with the healthy breathing pattern they normally take for granted. What is amazing is that as soon as they start to regain the healthy rhythm between inhaling and exhaling, everything starts to change. They may or may not climb any higher, but they always start to think more clearly and can make informed decisions. Ironically, they become more grounded.

I previously mentioned in the Introduction that I provide leadership to a 40-bed homeless shelter. Every Tuesday night, people from our shelter—a 50/50 mix of street-involved people and volunteers—go indoor rock climbing and have a great time together. Almost every week at least one or two people find themselves in the freak-out zone, and we see again and again the power that comes from telling a person to just breathe.

Personal Challenge—Breathing

I want you to take a minute and breathe with me. Let's take a few good deep breaths. *Inhale* for a count of three and then *exhale* for a count of three. Do it again. And one more time. Think about how with every breath you are inhaling the oxygen your body needs, and then as you exhale you are ridding the body of the built-up carbon dioxide.

Now, just for fun, let's pretend that we have decided that taking in oxygen is our biggest priority. Oxygen gives us energy, helps us think straight, keeps us active—who wouldn't want oxygen? So let's say we want to get all the oxygen we can—that we are just going to *inhale* for the rest of the day. We are taking an either/or approach and feeling that oxygen is the best solution to the breathing *problem*. Now, I want you to take a really deep breath and hold it for as long as you can.

You are feeling what happens, aren't you? Something does not feel right. Your body tells you that you need to exhale. Now!

If you decided that this whole inhaling thing was a really bad decision, that what you *really* needed to do to feel good was to e*xhale* for the rest of the day, as you would expect, that wouldn't work too well either.

I'm going to suggest that breathing is a great metaphor for healthy tension. If I treat breathing like a problem to solve and choose to *either* inhale *or* exhale as my "solution", I am guaranteed to end up in trouble. It might work for a little while, but before too long I will lose everything I set out to achieve...no question! I will end up blue in the face. However, if I can find a *healthy tension* between the *polarity* of *both* **inhaling** and **exhaling**, my body stays happy and healthy. That has us embracing the situation as a *polarity to manage* rather than a *problem to be solved*. And that makes all the difference.

HEALTHY BREATHING

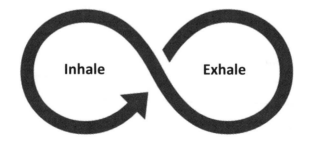

Polarities are Predictable

The encouraging news about polarities is that they are 100% pre-dictable. Once you have the ability to recognize that the challenge you are dealing with is a polarity to manage, how it looks and how it works will be the same every time and in every situation. Under-standing how a polarity looks and works gives us the ability to lev-erage it and achieve healthy tension.

> **Leverage**: (verb) To use something to maximum advantage.

A great way to start to understand the predictable nature of a polar-ity is for you to map out one that you manage every single day of your life—the polarity of *activity* and *rest*.

Personal Challenge—Mapping a Polarity

THRIVING
LIFE

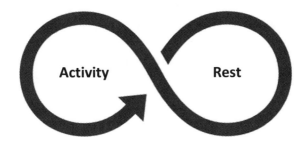

Activity   Rest

"Nature itself has a pulse, a rhythmic, wave-like movement between activity and rest. Think of the ebb and flow of the tides, the movement between seasons, and the daily rising and setting of the sun. Likewise, all organisms follow life-sustaining rhythms—birds migrating, bears hibernating, squirrels gathering nuts, and fish spawning, all of them at predictable rhythms. So, too, human beings are guided by

rhythms—both those dictated by nature and those encoded in our genes. We are oscillatory beings in an oscillatory universe. Rhythmicity is our inheritance."

Jim Loehr. *The Power of Full Engagement*

For the following exercise, take a piece of paper and draw four columns. I want you to think of as many positive results as you can for fully embracing **activity** in your life. When I refer to activity, I am not just talking about going to the gym. I want you to think about the word holistically—considering physical, emotional, intellectual, and spiritual activity; things like being healthy, energized, and opportunistic. List them in Column 1.

Next, I want you to think about the negative results that come from over-focusing on **activity** to the neglect of **rest**; things like burnout, injury, and stress. List them in Column 2.

Now, I want you to think of as many positive results as you can for fully embracing **rest** in your life. Again, when I say rest, I don't just mean having a nap. I mean things like peace, focus, and rejuvenation. List as many as you can in Column 3.

Finally—and I know this one is probably hard for busy folks to imagine—I want you to think about all the downsides that result from over-focusing on **rest** to the neglect of **activity**; things like boredom, depression, and apathy. List them in Column 4.

1. Positive
Results from
Focusing on
ACTIVITY

3. Positive
Results from
Focusing on
REST

2. Negative
Results from
Over-Focusing
on **ACTIVITY**
to the Neglect
of **REST**

4. Negative
Results from
Over-Focusing
on **REST**
to the Neglect
of **ACTIVITY**

As I said, polarities are incredibly predictable. The Activity/Rest exercise you just completed will give us a great opportunity to identify the key predictable elements not only for the polarity of activity and rest, but for every polarity you face in life.

Predictable Elements of a Polarity

1. **A polarity is unsolvable.** The first thing that is predictable about every polarity is that the situation is never going away. I will be managing the tension between **activity** and **rest** my entire life. The same is true for **structure** and **flexibility** in my parenting, and **inhaling** and **exhaling** to achieve healthy breathing. At times, I may manage the polarity better than at other times, but it's always going to be there. Understanding that polarities are unsolvable can be incredibly relieving. Once I accept this, I can stop beating myself up for failing to "solve" the problem, and I can instead commit myself to trying to do continually better at leveraging the tension.

2. **A polarity will always have two inseparable poles.** In this case, the poles are Activity and Rest. We use the term polarity because the two poles often feel like they are polar opposites. These poles are also referred to as conflicting values or different points of view, but *what is unique to the poles of a polarity is that the two sides of a polarity are inseparable over time.* One cannot exist in a healthy way without the other. For me to have a thriving life, I must embrace both **activity** *and* **rest**. In order to be an effective parent, I must embrace both **flexibility** *and* **structure**. In order to achieve healthy breathing, I must choose to both **inhale** *and* **exhale**.

3. **Each pole has a necessary "upside".** Each of the poles offers us things that are not only desirable, but are essential in our lives. If you look at the lists you wrote down in both Columns 1 and 3, many items on these lists are things you cannot live without.

4. **Each pole has a feared "downside"**. *When we choose one pole to the neglect of the opposite pole, we will inevitably end up living out the downside of that pole*. If I choose **activity** as my "solution" in life to the neglect of **rest**, I will lose all the great things I set out to achieve in Column 1, and will end up living out all the nasty things we see in Column 2, guaranteed!

When we realize that we are dealing with a polarity to manage, this mapping process allows us to see exactly what we are dealing with and to understand the dynamics of the tension we are facing. A map similar to what you just did with **activity** and **rest** can be done on a piece of paper, or even a napkin at a restaurant. A more formal and expansive mapping tool called a Polarity Map® was developed by Dr. Barry Johnson, who developed the concept of Polarity Thinking™. A copy of this Polarity Map® can be downloaded at www.thepowerofhealthytension.com/resources.

The following diagram will help you see the other predictable elements to all polarities:

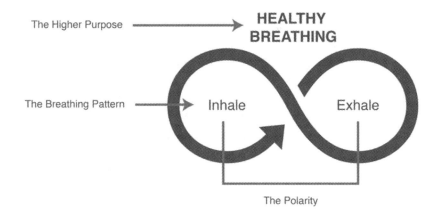

More Predictable Elements of a Polarity

5. **Every polarity serves a Higher Purpose**. The higher purpose in managing the tension between **activity** and **rest** is a **thriving life**. The goal of my previous parenting example was not to be **structured** or **flexible**. Instead, it was to find the best way to serve the higher purpose of being an **effective parent**. Similarly, **inhaling** and **exhaling** serve the higher purpose of **healthy breathing**. The more a person or team can achieve healthy tension between the two poles of a polarity, the more they will live out their higher purpose. The higher purpose answers the question, "*Why bother managing this tension?*" This is key to understanding why we need to manage the polarity, and why choosing to embrace tension is worthwhile.

6. **The Breathing Pattern**. I want you to notice one more thing about a polarity. When you look at the above diagram (and all the Healthy Tension illustrations), you will notice a "figure-eight". This is technically referred to as an Infinity Loop. However, throughout most of this book, I will simply refer to it as a Breathing Pattern. This illustrates the tension, or ongoing movement that exists between the two sides of a polarity. Our goal with any polarity—whether it be **activity** and **rest**, **structure** and **flexibility**, or other relevant tensions in your life—is that this looks like normal, healthy breathing. The objective of this book is for you to look at the tension that exists in the key polarities of your life, and determine if you are achieving healthy tension, similar to breathing. If it becomes apparent that the tension is quite unhealthy, we will then look at what can be done to get things back to a healthy place—just like breathing.

Now that we understand how predictable polarities are, let's look at how the polarity of **activity** and **rest** works in real life, using two different examples.

Activity and Rest Done Well

Quite a few years ago, a friend of mine, Jeff, gave me a challenge I couldn't refuse. Jeff was an accomplished long-distance runner who did a lot of coaching and personal training on the side. I had told him on a few occasions that I simply hadn't been born with the "running gene", and that no matter how much I tried, my high school gym class had proved to me that anything beyond a lap around the track was beyond my ability. Jeff strongly disagreed with my theory and challenged me, saying that if I'd be open to sticking to his training plan not only would I be able to do a few laps around the track, but that within six months I would be able to run a half-marathon. I took him up on his challenge because I knew that within no time he would come to the realization that he had massively miscalculated when it came to my running capabilities, and I would earn the right to a solid "I-told-you-so".

What was amazing to me, however, was what his training plan looked like. My assumption had been that if I was going to move from the couch to a half-marathon, I would just need to run more; that I would just have to push myself to keep going and going and going. But that wasn't the plan at all! To my surprise, Jeff's plan was every bit as strategic in terms of my need for rest and recovery as it was about my need for gains in distance. The only way to get to the end goal was to fully embrace **both activity** and **rest** in the days and months to come. If I overdid **activity** to the neglect of **rest**, I would end up injured; and if I overdid **rest** to the neglect of **activity**, my distance would not increase.

It turned out that Jeff was right and I was wrong. Up until that time, I had treated running as a problem to solve and not a polarity to manage. As a result, I had no idea of my own capabilities. I had underestimated myself. Not only did I run the half-marathon six months later, but since then I've run many more, as well as two full marathons.

This is a great example of a *virtuous cycle*. When the two poles (Activity and Rest) start to work off of one another in a healthy, reinforcing way, they create an energy system that moves the entire situation closer and closer to the Higher Purpose. This is the vision and the goal of any polarity that we are trying to manage.

Activity and Rest Done Not So Well

When I sold my consulting company in 2007, I had been living out of a suitcase and spending a considerable amount of my life on the road. The day the sale of the company was finalized, I decided I was going to take four months off. The thinking behind this strategy was that it would allow me to solve my problem of "just getting by" by fully embracing **rest**. I was going to sleep in, read some books, catch up on some must-see TV, and go for nice long walks. I was going to become everything I had not been able to be when I was consumed with work and constant travel.

I did all those things and it was great...for a while. But surprisingly, after about two weeks, I started to feel kind of sluggish. Then, after a month, a few courageous friends staged a bit of an intervention to tell me, "Dude, you're in a funk!" I had had the best of intentions with my strategy of not becoming an exhausted, overly-driven workaholic—but being a slug wasn't good either.

We refer to what I had done as the *pendulum effect*, and it is quite common. A person, team, or organization experiencing the "downside" of one pole starts to see the "upside" of the other pole as the solution. So they go there, but in time, due to treating the situation as a problem to be solved rather than a polarity to manage, they find that their solution isn't working because they are starting to lose everything they set out to achieve. When this happens, they wonder why they ever went there and yearn to go back to where they were in the first place. This happens over and over again, moving back and forth like a pendulum, spiraling people in a *vicious cycle*.

Even though I should have known better (based on polarity training), I was treating **activity** and **rest** as a problem to be solved, with **rest** being the "right" answer—and I ended up in a funk as a result. I was right in my strategy to add more rest and recreation to my life, but I was wrong to think that this would be a solution that would solve life's problems. The only way I would move toward my Higher Purpose of thriving in my life would be to do it in a way that fully embraced **rest**, but at the same time also fully embraced **activity.** I had to find a better way to hold these two conflicting values in healthy tension.

And I'm Not Talking about Balance

It is important to note that when I refer to Healthy Tension and managing polarities, I am not talking about simply finding balance. Balance assumes that there is a point where everything is in perfect alignment and our goal is to find that place and stay there as long as we can. The problem is that the tension that exists within a polarity is a living, breathing thing, and it's always changing. Therefore, there is never a point of perfect balance. What seemed balanced today may feel totally unbalanced tomorrow. I know in my own life that how I managed the polarity of **activity** and **rest** when I was single is completely different from how I manage it today, being married with two small kids. The Higher Purpose has always been the same (to thrive!), but how I achieve healthy tension needs to constantly change.

The term "balance" also can make it seem that a well-managed polarity has equally weighted sides, and that we are working towards a 50/50 outcome. This is not the case. A well-managed polarity might be heavily weighted towards one pole over the other. In parenting my son, I find that how I manage the **structure** and **flexibility** polarity is much more weighted on the **structure** side. He just seems to require more of that approach. With my daughter, on the other hand, I would say that I am managing this polarity best with a stronger emphasis on the **flexibility** pole. In both cases, it is far from a 50/50 split, and the proportions are always changing.

Why Polarity Thinking Matters

Let's return to the homeless shelter. As I mentioned, we did not really know what we were getting ourselves into when we agreed to take on the homeless shelter, but only days after saying yes, we had about 60 people living in our church building, so we quickly had to get our heads around what that meant. The great thing was that right from day one, our core group of staff, volunteers, and homeless residents were incredibly unified on our core values: we wanted to be a community of **LOVE,** a community of **FAIRNESS**, and a community that embodied the healthy qualities of **HOME**. There was no debate—we were totally aligned on these values.

SOUTHRIDGE SHELTER

Core Values

And yet, if I were to ask how we should go about living out these values, it would often split the community right in half. Someone would argue that FAIRNESS meant being consistent and making sure we treated everyone equally—but then someone else would push back and say, "Wait a minute, not everyone has the same abilities. FAIRNESS isn't making sure everyone gets the same thing—it's that everyone gets what they need."

At times, the banter and push-back we had debating our differences in interpretation was fun, but when it came to dealing with situations that really mattered, and when push came to shove (and fortunately it never literally came to pushing and shoving), we realized that we had a polarized team. We found that our three core values were about as useless as those cheesy motivational posters you used to see in the 1980s that said things like Team-work, Passion and Leadership (often with an eagle or a waterfall in the background). *The words on the wall didn't match the walk down the hall.*

What changed everything was when we started to realize that these three values were in fact each Higher Purposes, and with each one came an underlying polarity that we had to acknowledge, and find a way to achieve healthy tension between the two poles.

SOUTHRIDGE SHELTER

Core Values

Underlying Tensions

We really wanted to offer LOVE, FAIRNESS, and HOME, but the reality was that unless we were willing to embrace healthy tension, we were never going to be about those things.

Let me give you an example of the tensions we faced. I mentioned that one of our core values was LOVE (which we now call a Higher Purpose). Even before I started working at the shelter, I was quite involved in street outreach. It all started for me when one day I had an unexpected conversation with a guy named Wayne. Wayne spent most of his life on the streets, and it had taken a significant toll on him physically, mentally, and emotionally. Wayne also had a crippling drug addiction. On many levels, Wayne and I were quite different, yet surprisingly on many more levels we found that we were incredibly similar. Within a short amount of time Wayne became one of my best friends and one of the biggest teachers in my life.

When I learned about Wayne's life, it became clear to me that the one thing he had never experienced in life was **unconditional acceptance**—love and friendship that came without strings or judgment. Something that I often took for granted in my life was that in spite of making some really bad decisions now and then, I always knew that I had friends and family in my corner. I never had to question if I would have people there for me to provide love, acceptance, and support. Seeing that this had never been the case for Wayne, I thought that if somehow I could just be there for him, regardless of how well or how poorly he did—if I could just love and support him in a way that unconditionally accepted him as a person—there might be a chance that this could give him the encouragement and confidence he needed to be able to get out of his desperate situation.

So that was my strategy in trying to "solve the problem" of Wayne's homelessness. I would be unconditionally accepting. I was going to be there for him, no matter what he had done, no matter what he did. I wasn't going anywhere. To the best of my ability, I would not judge him. I would just be there. And it worked…for a while.

Over the course of the next few months, I saw an incredible change in Wayne's life. Not only was he able to move off the streets, but he also had new job opportunities, he began addressing his addiction issues, and he even started to reach out to estranged family members. Although this positive change could be attributed to a number of things, I definitely saw the "upside" of **unconditional acceptance** being lived out in Wayne's life.

However, as we learned with our breathing example, when we choose one side of a polarity to the neglect of the other, we eventually lose the things we set out to achieve, and inevitably start to experience the downside of our approach. I learned the hard way that by only caring and relating to Wayne in an unconditionally accepting way, I was actually hurting him. I was not allowing him to experience the consequences of his behavior. I was not challenging Wayne to live up to his potential. I had become an enabler, and things started to fall off the rails. In time, Wayne's progress started to slow and he started to move back into the same old patterns and behaviors that worked against his recovery.

What I began to realize (the hard way) was that the only way I could live out my higher purpose of LOVE in Wayne's life was to be able to be unconditionally accepting *while at the same time* holding Wayne accountable. My preference towards **unconditional acceptance** (gentle love) was actually dangerous when not held in tension with **accountability** (tough love).

LOVE

Unconditional
Acceptance

Accountability

I should add that when it comes to the choice between **unconditional acceptance** and **accountability**, I still like to be on the **unconditional acceptance** side. For me, it is a much more comfortable place. I've learned (and I'm learning) that if I can somehow live in healthy tension and hold on to the gentle love of **unconditional acceptance**, but in a way that also embraces the tough love of **accountability**, my life has the potential of being used in a powerful way.

My friendship and experience with Wayne is just one example from countless others I could have offered. It has become clear to us in our work at the homeless shelter that if we really mean what we say in wanting to live out our higher purposes of LOVE, FAIRNESS, and HOME, we need to be prepared to live in each of their underlying tensions every single day. These three polarities possess the breathing pattern that brings our three higher purposes to life. The only way we can live out our mission and vision is to acknowledge and embrace healthy tension in our community.

It's Hard Work...But Worth It!

Managing polarities and pursuing healthy tension is hard work! There is a great quote from the writer F. Scott Fitzgerald who said *"The test of a first-rate intelligence is the ability to hold two opposed ideas in the mind at the same time and still retain the ability to function."* It's kind of like when we were kids and we would try to rub our stomachs while patting our heads at the same time: it's just easier to do one thing. We often feel better and more confident when we can focus only on one thing. As a parent, I sometimes wish I could just be **structured; flexibility** is somewhat uncomfortable for me. In life, I prefer to fully embrace **activity** and not put too much thought or energy into **rest**. When we have to do two things at the same time, it is harder and more complex. We feel more vulnerable and we yearn for a simple answer.

Rarely do I leave a staff meeting at the shelter without the team debating or arguing about the same old issues—how to live out the values of LOVE, FAIRNESS, and a HOME in a real way. We have accepted that these are unsolvable challenges that we face, and that the only way we can live out our higher purposes of LOVE, FAIRNESS, and HOME is by leaning in and embracing their underlying tensions.

I know in my workplace this can, at times, drive a person crazy. It can be exhausting dealing with these chronic issues over and over again. Managing polarities and pursuing healthy tension is hard work. But it's worth it! I am reminded just how worthwhile it is every time I look at this photograph.

The photo was taken at a sports camp during one of our shelter retreats. Every year, we gather close to a hundred former residents from our homeless shelter and go up north for a weekend together. It's kind of like the summer camp most of these folks have never had the chance to experience. We have fun with our cabin teams, play games, have parties, and celebrate the amazing community of which we get to be a part.

One of the women in the picture, the one who looks as though she's howling with laughter, had been in 17 group homes by the time she was 16. That is when she decided to live on the streets, because it was a better option than what she had been going home to. Along the way, she had three children and had all of them taken away from her; she struggled with extreme addiction and mental health challenges, and ultimately ended up working in the sex trade. Today, she has graduated from college, has her kids back, and is a real leader and poverty advocate in our community. The rest of the women in the circle have diverse stories, but with equal parts tragedy and transformation.

I look at this picture often to remind myself that our higher purposes *are* being lived out and *are* saving lives. And the *only* way we can live out these higher purposes of LOVE, FAIRNESS, and HOME is to have the courage to wrestle each and every day with their underlying polarities. As leaders and as a team, we must have the resolve to constantly pursue healthy tension.

Pictures like this do not happen unless people are willing to live in tension. It would be easier to deal with things from a good/bad and right/wrong perspective and to treat homelessness as if it were a problem to be solved. We could just avoid the tensions altogether. But ultimately, if we truly want to be about LOVE, FAIRNESS, and HOME, and if we want to see people find hope and healing in their very broken lives, we have to be willing to embrace the tensions of our core polarities.

Within a week or two of walking through the doors of our shelter, we orient all of our new staff and volunteers to these three higher purposes and their underlying polarities. We forewarn them that they will literally run into these tensions every single day they are in the shelter. We prepare them to understand that they will see decisions made that they might not understand and at times might really struggle with. But we go on to explain that *healthy tension is the business that we are in,* that if we are not open to dealing with polarizing perspectives, and are not prepared to live in tension each and every day, we should probably close our doors. We are only able to live our higher purposes—and see more pictures like the one on page 35—if we have the courage and resolve to embrace these tensions each and every day. It is hard work...and it's worth it!

SECTION TWO

Application

Application

Now that we are aware of polarities and healthy tension, I'm going to introduce you to a simple four-step framework that will allow you to tap into the power of healthy tension—both at work and home.

THE POWER OF HEALTHY TENSION

IDENTIFY YOUR CRUX TENSION	**MIND YOUR BIAS**	**LEARN THE LANGUAGE**	**MAKE INFORMED DECISIONS**
Seeing is relieving	Embrace your opposite	There is wisdom in resistance	Go slow to go fast

Step 1: Identify Your Crux Tensions

**IDENTIFY YOUR
CRUX TENSION**

Seeing is
relieving

If the only thing you do with this book is implement Step One of this four-step framework, I am confident that this alone will be well worth your time and energy, and have a significant impact in your life. This step is huge!

Something that often happens right about now in your pursuit of embracing healthy tension is that you start to see polarities everywhere. You start to realize that we deal with a long list of conflicting values in our work, at home, and in our relationships. This can create a bit of polarity paranoia, leaving you feeling overwhelmed. But rest assured, there are two key reasons that everything is going to be okay:

- The first reason is that you have been dealing with tensions your entire life. From the moment you entered this world and took your first breath, you have been dealing with a countless number of dilemmas, paradoxes, and conflicting values. There is not a day that goes by when you are not managing tensions that include work vs. home, activity vs. rest, structure vs. flexibility, and many others. My guess is that you have probably been doing a decent job at it or you wouldn't have gotten this far.

- The second reason is that at the end of the day, you do not actually need to pay much attention to the myriad of tensions you are dealing with—you really only need to worry about a few crux tensions. Let me explain.

**Southridge Shelter
Rock-Climbing Program in Action**

Back when I had a lot more free time and a lot less responsibility, I did quite a bit of rock climbing. This would often result in my friends and I doing trips to renowned rock-climbing areas across North America. We would research the area in advance so that when we got there, we would know the best climbs to attempt. Once we found these renowned climbs, there would normally be a few local climbers around. We would immediately ask them to help us identify the "crux moves" on the climb, because we knew that between where we stood on the ground and where we wanted to get to at the top of the cliff, there might be hundreds of moves that we would need to do—but there were probably only one or two moves that really mattered. They were the make-it-or-break-it moves that would be the gatekeepers to our success. And we found that if someone could help us identify these few crux moves—and we put most of our effort and energy into anticipating, understanding, and trying to conquer them—the other fifty to a hundred moves would pretty much take care of themselves.

A similar phenomenon is true with managing tensions. The reality is that there are hundreds, maybe thousands of tensions and conflicting values that you deal with at work, at home, and in your relationships. As I previously said, for the most part you are probably doing just fine in dealing with these tensions. However, there are typically two or three that really matter. These are the polarities that you find yourself dealing with every single day; tensions that always seem to be tied to how well or poorly things are going. The conflicts that have you (and your teammates) saying, "I can't believe we're dealing with this again". We will refer to these as your *crux tensions*, and I would suggest that they are the gatekeepers to your ability to thrive.

I explained earlier that I have come to realize that a crux tension in my parenting is the ability to find healthy tension between **structure** and **flexibility**. Although we deal with hundreds of tensions every day in the homeless shelter, we have found that there are only three we really need to keep focused on:

- the crux tension of **unconditional acceptance** and **accountability** to pursue our higher purpose of LOVE;

- **consistency** and **individuality** to pursue our higher purpose of FAIRNESS; and

- **fun** and **seriousness** to pursue our higher purpose of HOME.

When we put specific focus and energy into managing these three crux tensions, we get better at managing tensions in general, and find that most of the time the rest of the long list of tensions that exist seem to take care of themselves.

Taking the time to identify the crux tensions that you face at work and at home will be absolutely game-changing.

Personal Challenge: Identify Your Crux Tension

Look through the list of common tensions on the following page. Some of them are organizationally focused, others are more leadership oriented, and some relate more to life in general. You might find that you resonate with a lot of the different tensions, but I want you to narrow this down and select the one that resonates the most; the one you would identify as make-it or break-it tension for you to manage. This will be the tension that you have the most energy around. In other words, you are looking to identify your crux tension. Do not worry about whether you are managing this tension particularly well or particularly poorly, just take note of the one that you find yourself dealing with every day; a chronic issue that arises again and again. You may find that there are two or three, as opposed to one. Take note of all of them, but for the rest of this book, just focus on the one that stands out the most.

Take some time to decide and then circle this tension on the following page.

Common Tensions

- Task Focused **AND** Relationship Oriented
- Truthful & Candid **AND** Tactful & Diplomatic**
- Data Driven **AND** People Driven*
- Directive **AND** Participative
- Control **AND** Empowerment
- Critical Analysis **AND** Encouragement*
- Conditional Respect **AND** Unconditional Respect*
- Give Freedom **AND** Hold Accountable*
- Confidence **AND** Humility
- Grounded **AND** Visionary
- Structure **AND** Flexibility
- Planning **AND** Execution
- Logic **AND** Gut-Feeling**

- Care for My Part of the Organization **AND** Care for the Whole Organization*
- Centralized Coordination **AND** Decentralized Initiatives*
- Diverse Individuals **AND** Unified Team*
- Competing with Others **AND** Collaborating with Others
- Recognize the Individual **AND** Recognize the Team
- Manage Costs **AND** Maintain Quality
- Preserve Tradition & Stability **AND** Stimulate Innovation & Change**
- Focus on Short Term **AND** Focus on Long Term
- Deep Understanding **AND** Simplicity**
- Mission **AND** Margin*
- Care for Self **AND** Care for Others
- Work **AND** Home

*Thanks to Dr. Barry Johnson, Polarity Management Associates
**Thanks to Jim Collins, *Good to Great*

Questions about your Crux Tension:

1. Make a list of ways you experience this tension on a regular basis, how it challenges you, and where it surfaces.

2. How well are you doing in managing this tension?

3. Who else impacts how well or poorly this tension is managed?

4. If others impact the management of this tension, are they aware of the role they play? How clear and open are you in talking about the tension with them?

5. What would it take to manage this tension better in the future?

Seeing is Relieving

When I talk about identifying your crux tensions, I often say that "seeing is relieving." When we can identify the key tensions that we are constantly wrestling with, we normally experience a huge amount of relief. The night that our friends left our home after the parenting conversation, my wife and I felt an incredible sense of relief because we were finally able to identify and understand the key tension and challenge that we were up against. Although we realized that tension between **structure** and **flexibility** was never going to go away, and that there was no one *right* answer to our parenting challenge, we were encouraged to know that regardless of what all the books, websites, and testimonials claimed, no one else out there has ever "solved" the problem of parenting either. *Phew!* It wasn't a problem that we would ever solve.

In the homeless shelter, this allowed us to breathe a sigh of relief as well, realizing that it was okay that we were dealing with these ongoing tensions every day—in fact it was *important* that we embraced them. Now, when we are divided about how we do things in our shelter, the identification and understanding of our crux tension provides us with a common language that helps to defuse the situation and navigate the way forward in a healthy way. It shows us that we are at odds and feeling tension for good reasons. It helps us pinpoint what we need to train our staff and volunteers in, and how these tensions need to be acknowledged and integrated into any work plans or change initiatives. Identifying and focusing on achieving healthy tension in our crux polarities has allowed us to start to *walk our talk.*

Application

SOUTHRIDGE SHELTER

Core Values

Underlying Tensions

Step 2: Mind Your Bias

**IDENTIFY YOUR
CRUX TENSION**

Seeing is
relieving

**MIND
YOUR BIAS**

Embrace your
opposite

When you look at the above picture what do you see? Do you see the rabbit? Or do you see the duck? My guess is that you are able to see both, but I bet you were able to see one picture more quickly than the other. And even though you know that there are two pictures in one, every time you look you will still see one first and a little bit more clearly. This would be an example of a "bias." A bias is our preference—or our default point of view. It's what we see first and what we see the clearest.

I am going to suggest that with every tension you manage, you will *always* have a bias to one side over the other. Much like the example of the duck and the rabbit, you will see and understand one pole of the polarity more clearly than the other. This doesn't necessarily mean that you like one side and dislike the other, or that you believe that one side is right and the other side is wrong. It simply means that we all have a preference. Sometimes this is a very strong bias and other times it will be a subtle one—but having a bias is a fact of life.

We might resist the idea of bias, thinking we are above that and that we always see things from a completely objective point of view. I am going to suggest, however, that this is a faulty and dangerous assumption. **Having a bias isn't necessarily good or bad in itself—it just** *is.* As I told you in my experience with my friend Wayne, I tend to approach things from the pole of **unconditional acceptance** rather than **accountability**. That is clearly my bias. And because of this bias, I will easily identify and value the "upsides" of my preferred pole *and* easily identify and fear the downsides of the opposite pole.

Having a bias is not a bad thing; in fact, it can be a very positive thing. But our bias is either working for us or against us. **The goal when dealing with a tension is to** *mind* **your bias.** Similar to "minding your manners", or "minding the gap" (if you have traveled in the UK), "minding your bias" means to pay attention to it; to be aware of it; and to be *mindful* of it. This means to have both *confidence and humility* based on your bias. Confidence comes from knowing that we possess a unique point of view, potentially a point of view that no one else totally sees or understands. We want to take responsibility for bringing this unique point of view to our work, our homes, our teams, and our relationships. Humility comes from knowing that there is always a different—yet equally true—point of view. This diverse point of view is one that we might not be able to see clearly, or even see at all, without the help of others. When we mind our bias, and we practice both confidence and humility, our bias can be a beautiful and powerful thing. However, when biases are not minded and our points of view are taken as the *best* answer or the *whole* truth, they can be quite dangerous and damaging (for us and those around us).

Personal Challenge: Identifying Bias

Let's look for a moment at our own biases using the tension of **individual approach** vs. **team approach**. I want you to put an "X" somewhere on the spectrum below, based on where your preference lies. If you prefer to accomplish a task through independence, personal ownership, and responsibility, you will put your X somewhere on the Individual Approach side. If you feel like you are at your best when you are working with other people and getting things done in a collaborative environment, you will place your X somewhere on the side of Team Approach.

Individual Approach	5	4	3	2	1	1	2	3	4	5	Team Approach

Now, let's examine your bias:

- Why do you prefer the side you chose?
- What about the other side do you fear or resist?
- How do you capitalize on the unique point of view that your bias allows you to bring to your work and home?
- Do you ever feel that you get into trouble by overdoing this bias to the neglect of the other side?

If your choice is more on the **individual** side, the reason for your preference might be that you are more introverted, that you had a bad experience in groups, or that you enjoy the creative process of developing an idea by yourself. There are many possible reasons, some of which come from nurture and others from nature. The same is true if you lean towards the **team** side. Maybe you know that you think best aloud, or you have had amazing experiences with teamwork, or appreciate hearing multiple points of view.

Let's do the same exercise around **truthful & candid** vs. **tactful & diplomatic**. If you place your "X" somewhere on the **tactful & diplomatic** side, it would suggest that when you are having a conversation, you pay more attention to the relationship and how what you say is being received. Someone who leans more toward the **truthful & candid** side would be more focused on being clear and making sure what needs to be said gets said—calling a spade a spade. Put your X on the line for where you most prefer to operate.

Truthful &											Tactful &
Candid	5	4	3	2	1	1	2	3	4	5	Diplomatic

Now, let's examine this bias as well:

- Why do you prefer the side you chose?
- What about the other side do you fear or resist?
- How do you capitalize on the unique point of view that your bias allows you to bring to your work and home?
- Do you ever feel that you get into trouble by overdoing this bias to the neglect of the other side?

Minding Your Bias

In terms of minding your bias, I have found that there are two important steps:

1. First, simply *acknowledge your bias*—identify what is clearest and most comfortable for you, and be able to articulate this to others. This is most important when it comes to your crux tension because that is a polarity you deal with every day, and you need to know whether your bias is working for or against you.

2. Second, search out and team up with someone who shares the same higher purpose as you, but when it comes to your crux tension their bias is the polar opposite of yours. If you don't recognize the benefit someone with an opposite bias can provide, that kind of person can become a thorn in your side and drive you crazy. However, if you are able to see the wisdom that

comes from their resistance and embrace their different perspective, they can become a powerful and important ally as you work together to achieve your higher purpose together. We call this *embracing your opposite.*

Let me give you an example. My personal bias in the **truthful & candid** vs. **tactful & diplomatic** tension is very strong on the **truthful & candid** side. I can think of many ways this bias has been positive in terms of my leadership and what I bring to the organization. However, it can be a dangerous thing if I am not deliberate about minding it. If I'm working on a potentially controversial email that I plan to send to my whole team at work, because of my bias towards **candor** I have learned that I often benefit from a second set of eyes on the email before it goes out. However, what I'm inclined to do is to run it by someone who is a lot like me and shares my **candid** bias. And you can guess what happens when I do that: they agree with me and congratulate me on such a well-written email. As a result, I feel great and press SEND. You can also guess what happens next: the email causes a blowup in our team and the negative impact is a million miles away from my positive intent. For the most part, that is my fault because I did not seek the perspective of someone who has a different bias from me. By aligning with someone who shares my **candid** bias, I just reinforce it rather than searching out someone with a **tactful & diplomatic** bias to get a more diverse perspective that would help me to see things from a different and valuable point of view.

This isn't just something to keep in mind with our teams at work; it is important in other aspects of our lives as well. Think of how this impacts our political preferences. If I'm someone who has a somewhat liberal bias, I am likely to watch liberal-leaning news stations, read those types of articles, and "like" comments on Facebook that affirm my liberal point of view. Slowly but surely, I can surround myself with likeminded perspectives, making me vulnerable to mistaking my bias for the whole truth. The same is true if I lean more towards a conservative bias. This is an unfortunate reality, resulting in polarization, blind spots, and close-mindedness.

Instead of creating a world where we are constantly reinforcing our bias, the most powerful and courageous thing we can do is seek out other people (and news sources) that offer alternative perspectives, and learn to benefit and grow from the inevitable tension that this will provide.

I have learned (the hard way!) that it is crucial for me to search out someone who has very different biases from me, and to be open to their point of view. When thinking of the recent example of **truthful & candid** vs. **tactful & diplomatic**, I can think of many times when I sought out a **tactful & diplomatic** biased person to look over an email I felt great about and had them say to me, *"You were actually going to send that?!"* Based on their bias, they will easily see how the impact of my email is not in line with my intent. They can help me frame things differently, or may even suggest that this message is not one to be sent by email, but rather needs a face-to-face conversation.

Embracing Your Opposite

"It's always wise to seek the truth in our opponents' error, and the error in our own truth."

Niebuhr

What does it mean to embrace your opposite? Let me start by telling you what it doesn't mean: tolerance. In our country, we strongly value tolerance, and I believe that tolerance can be a useful skill. However, when it comes to tensions, tolerance does not go far enough. Tolerance is defined as "enduring without repugnance", which means that we learn to co-exist or put up with each other. When it comes to embracing my opposite, tolerance will not cut it. The only way we can start to benefit from the healthy tension that exists from an alternative point of view is when we are able to not simply tolerate that view, but actually embrace it.

If I am really going to mind my bias, I have to move way beyond tolerance to *embrace* my opposite—a word that literally translates to "hug". That doesn't mean you need to physically give your coworker a bear hug, but you do need to fully embrace their point of view. Instead of just listening and tolerating the other person's point of view, embracing your opposite means that you are striving to understand and are open to integrating their perspective, especially when it appears to be the polar opposite of yours. You live with the assumption that you often only see the tip of the iceberg, so you will work hard to see what lies beneath the surface—the part you are missing.

Moving from tolerating to embracing is easier said than done. In my email example, when I get perspective from someone with a **tactful & diplomatic** bias, I have to be careful not to simply "sell" my rationale to them and argue the intention of my email. I also have to be careful not to get defensive if they have concerns about what I have written. Embracing your opposite is always worth the hard (and humbling) work. I might read an email over and over and be fine with it, but a person with an opposite bias is able to point things out that I never intended to say, and show me the blindspots created by my biases. When I have the discipline to embrace the additional point of view my colleague is offering and explore how our two perspectives can work together, not only do I often land on a much better solution, I also avoid unnecessary blowups with my team.

Once I am clear on the biases I hold in my crux tensions, I need to learn the importance of deliberately teaming up with people who see things in a way that is opposite to my point of view. These are people I trust and who are aligned with me on higher purposes, but who almost always approach things in a totally different way.

Although it is easier and more comfortable to connect with people who share my point of view, it is these alternative views I lean on when dealing with new and challenging situations. I try to give these people free rein to call me on what they see happening, so that they can unabashedly offer their perspective about how to approach a situation. These are the people who challenge me rather than just accept my point of view. They have become a safe and valued resource for me to see things in a more complete way, and to consider an approach that brings both sides of a tension into play; an approach I otherwise would have missed out on.

When Bias Works against Us

"A point of view can be a dangerous luxury when substituted for insight and understanding."

Marshall McLuhan

Let me give you a personal example of when my bias was working against me and hurting those around me. As I mentioned earlier, one of the crux tensions in our homeless shelter is the polarity of HOME. On one hand, we need to embrace the pole of **seriousness**, knowing we deal with significant issues every day, and that for some of the people we serve these issues can literally be a matter of life and death. On the other hand, we also believe that a HOME is about smiling, laughing, and enjoying community together—the pole of **fun**. When it comes to this crux tension, I have a strong bias towards **fun,** and as a result I think that I have been able to bring a lot of value to our community. We have fun recreational programs every night that range from card tournaments to indoor rock climbing to creative arts workshops. We celebrate birthdays and recovery milestones. We sing karaoke. By focusing on the pole of **fun**, we have been able to tap into a glimmer of hope and joy that the streets have often beaten down in the people we serve (and sometimes in those of us who are doing the serving).

HOME

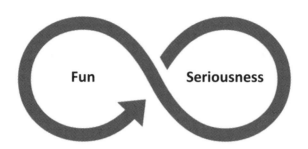

As a leader, I understand that for us to be a HOME, we need to manage the tension between **fun** and **seriousness**, and I totally see value on both sides. However, because my bias towards **fun** is so strong, it is easy for this bias to work against me (and our organization).

A couple of years ago, around Easter, we had a woman staying at the shelter who loved making crafts. In the weeks leading up to Easter, she transformed the place by decorating it with lovely Easter crafts. Everywhere you looked there were baskets, bunnies, and eggs. I looked around a few days before Easter weekend and I thought, "This is great. I bet there isn't another shelter in the country that's embracing fun like we do."

That same day, a gentleman from the streets who was staying with us asked if he could talk to me for a few minutes. I could tell from the tone of his voice that what he had to talk about mattered so we found some private space for the conversation. He explained that he understood why we as a shelter would embrace the Easter season, and even acknowledged the benefit in celebrating the way we did. But, he went on to request that at least a corner of the shelter be free from the decorations so that they were not constantly reminding him that he wasn't going to be spending Easter with his kids. His words hit me like a ton of bricks. As soon as he said it, I thought, "Of course!" I wondered how I could have missed something so obvious. It was a humbling reminder for me in that moment; my bias towards **fun** wasn't serving the organization well, and the tension around our greater purpose of HOME was far from being managed in a healthy way.

I had the experience to know that we were dealing with a polarity to manage (not a problem to solve), not that we needed to tear down all the decorations and declare no more celebrating in the future. It was just a humbling indicator that we were not doing a good job of achieving healthy tension in our management of the polarity of **fun** and **seriousness**. We needed to deal with this tension a whole lot better.

I met with our team that day and told them about the conversation and my realization that we were not managing the polarity of HOME very well. At that meeting, two staff members sheepishly said they had been thinking the same thing, but had not mentioned it. That was a second wake-up call for me, because it is not a healthy sign when team members who have different points of view feel that they cannot express them. It made me aware that as a leader, my bias can easily be a trump card—but that does not serve the organization or its higher purposes at all. It made me realize the need for a leader, more than anyone, to "embrace their opposite" in order to manage key polarities well, not just at Easter but all the time.

Similar to the duck/rabbit picture, the image above also contains two pictures in one. My guess is that you saw the face first, and that it took a bit more work to see the word "LIAR". In fact, if I didn't mention that the word LIAR existed in this picture, it's possible you might not have seen it at all. This is often the case when it comes to bias. I can understand that there are two sides to a polarity, but unless someone with a different perspective helps me see the other point of view, I may not have the ability to see it on my own. We need to seek out that kind of help and embrace this complementary perspective when we are dealing with polarities that matter to us at work and at home.

When it comes to the crux tensions, we often have strongly-held biases, so it is really important for us to identify and *mind* these biases. A bias can be a great thing when you leverage it for the benefit of your work, your team, and your relationships—so long as you are not convinced that your bias is the right answer, the *most right* answer, or the only answer.

Personal Challenge: Mind Your Bias

Think about the crux tension you identified on page 44. What is your bias within your crux tension? Write in the poles of your crux tension below, and put an "X" on the spectrum indicating your bias.

Left Pole ----------------------------------|---------------------------------- **Right Pole**
        5   4   3   2   1 | 1   2   3   4   5

Now, let's examine your bias:

- In what ways is this bias working for you or against you at work and at home?

- When it comes to this crux tension, can you identify someone who would be "your opposite" in that they are working toward the same higher purpose as you, but have the total opposite bias to yours?

- Are you embracing your opposite and taking advantage of their diverse perspective? Are there ways you could do a better job of embracing your opposite?

Step 3: Learn the Language

IDENTIFY YOUR CRUX TENSION	**MIND YOUR BIAS**	**LEARN THE LANGUAGE**
Seeing is relieving	Embrace your opposite	There is wisdom in resistance

So, you are grasping this idea of *healthy tension*. You have identified a crux tension, something that is make-it-or-break-it in your life. You have acknowledged the fact that you have a bias toward one side of this polarity over the other. You have sought out someone with an opposite point of view from yours and are committed to embracing this person's unique perspective. Now the real challenge is: how do you have a productive conversation with this person and not just end up in a polarizing debate about who is right and who is wrong?

This is a critical stage in the process, because if you are anything like me these types of conversations do not come naturally. As I said earlier, my mother tongue is problem solving. I like to banter and debate in a way that pulls from an either/or, good/bad, right/wrong paradigm. A problem-solving approach is my default. However, the unfortunate reality is that if I engage in conversation with a person whose bias is opposite to mine, using problem-solving tactics and language, it will inevitably drive the other person more strongly into their bias, and we will end up more polarized than we were before the conversation.

There has never been a time that we are seeing the negative impact of these polarizing conversations more than right now. With the political right and left more divided than they have ever been before, and people affirming their biases and beliefs through what they choose to watch and read, our society is finding it harder and harder to have positive conversations with people who do not share our points of view. And it's not just politics; people are divided on issues like economic development vs. environmental protection; opening our borders to refugees vs. homeland security; and celebrating cultural difference vs. preserving a national identity. Families that used to be able to have healthy dialogue around the dinner table have stopped talking about controversial subjects. Workplaces have deemed certain topics "off limits" for conversation due to people's inability to navigate their different points of view. We are losing our ability to talk about our differences in a healthy way.

We have to have a different kind of conversation! We have to learn to speak the language of Polarity Management. And for me, this is often a struggle. This is not my first language, and I have to be quite deliberate about doing things differently. However, it is a powerful language that I'm continually learning, taking my ability to communicate to a higher level.

Communication Crisis

Here is an example to illustrate the need for a different kind of conversation: In our homeless shelter, FAIRNESS is another of our crux tensions. We are strongly aligned in our belief that everyone who walks through our door should feel and experience FAIRNESS. However, in spite of everyone being in agreement with this higher purpose, the way in which we should live it out is often highly debated.

FAIRNESS

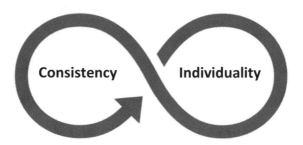

Within our staff and volunteer team, there are people who see **consistency** as the best way to get to FAIRNESS. These are often our Resident Service Managers (RSMs) who are responsible for overseeing the floor and who work hard at making sure that every day our 40 homeless residents, staff, and volunteers all get along and live well together. They recognize that we need to avoid favoritism and inconsistencies in how we operate in order to avoid chaos and confusion. They also remind us that many of the people who stay with us are in addiction recovery, and for these people **consistency** is foundational to safety and security.

There are other staff members who believe that FAIRNESS does not necessarily mean that people get the same treatment, but instead that everyone gets what they need. They know that each person has their own story and their own ability level, which can even vary from day to day. These folks champion **individuality**. That's their bias. Some of our team members have the role of a coach and work one-on-one with our residents. These coaches often hold this **individuality** bias. Through their personal connection with each person, they can clearly see how everyone needs to be treated in a way that is appropriate for them—and that what is appropriate and fair for one person is not necessarily appropriate for another.

Application

Our RSMs and our coaches normally envision a community of FAIR-NESS lived out in diverse ways, and often talk about these conflicting biases in staff meetings, even joking about them at times. But every now and then we are faced with a situation that is incredibly serious, that truly polarizes the team, and all of a sudden these diverging perspectives are no longer a laughing matter.

We had such an experience a year ago when a young woman staying with us made the decision to use an illegal substance that is not allowed on our property. This resulted in a fight within our team. The RSMs—our **consistency**-biased folks—argued that it was obvious that the result of this woman's decision was suspension, and that we would work with her to find a suitable place for her to stay for a few nights. They reminded us that this suspension was needed for a few reasons: first, it was important that this woman experience the consequences of her decision, that a suspension was the "tough love" required for her to make better decisions in the future. Second, we had to consider the other residents in our shelter, many of whom had come to our facility to get away from this kind of drug culture. The RSMs argued that if we were not consistent with our guidelines and did not enact a suspension, we would enable the woman, trigger drug use in others, and tarnish the reputation of our shelter as being a safe, clean place.

This made perfect sense to me until the person who was the coach of this young woman spoke up. She explained how she had been working with this young woman for many months, and that the progress in her life was nothing short of a miracle. And even more, the coach told us that the next day this young woman was being admitted to a drug treatment program, an opportunity that doesn't happen easily in our area. Her coach passionately argued that if we ended up suspending this woman, there was zero chance that she would be going to the drug treatment program. There was also no guarantee that we would see her again—ever. This could be a life-or-death decision.

All of a sudden, we found ourselves in what I call a *tug-of-war con-versation*. This occurs when we get locked into either/or thinking, and become more and more entrenched on our own side, while desperately trying to persuade others to embrace our point of view. We had two camps, the **consistency** camp and the **individuality** camp. Both sides had valid perspectives, yet conversation was escalating into a conflict that was not healthy on any level. The more we debated, the more polarized the two camps became.

Finally, I was forced to call a "time out". We had to recognize that this young woman deserved a better conversation than the one we were having, and we needed to treat each other with a lot more respect than we were currently giving one another. We needed to approach the situation (and one another) differently. We had to stop acting as if the situation was an either/or problem to solve, and instead embrace the fact that it was incredibly complex and required both/and thinking and the language of polarity management.

Tug-of-War Conversations

Can you relate to the tug-of-war conversation I explained above? Can you think of situations in your life where you feel that you are digging in deep, holding on to your side of the rope, and are determined to pull others over? I don't want to suggest that a tug-of-war conversation is wrong all the time. There are certain problem-solving situations where it *is* important for me to get people to the other side. I can think of times at the homeless shelter when a staff member was failing to implement a policy that was in place to keep people safe. When dealing with a situation like this, it is my job to explain what needs to happen and "pull" the person over to my side. I am right and they are wrong. But when I'm faced with a polarity and the situation is not so simple, a tug-of-war approach will increase the conflict and lead to unnecessary pain.

If I am having a tug-of-war conversation when dealing with a polarity, my approach to the conversation will be predictable. I will start by explaining the "upside" of my point of view and then talk about the "downside" of the opposite point of view.

The RSMs who had a strong bias toward **consistency** would tell our coaches why consistency was the *right* approach, and then would explain the slippery slope that would result from embracing **individuality**.

A CONSISTENCY POINT OF VIEW

- Creates a safe, structured, and predictable environment that is critical for recovery
- Ensures that everyone is treated equally and objectively
- Protects the values and needs of the greater community

- Fails to provide the structure and consistency needed in the recovery journey
- People question their value in the community due to real or perceived favoritism
- Neglects the values and needs of the greater community

When the RSMs were finished talking, they would assume that the coaches would see how obvious their argument was and would change their point of view. But instead, they experienced resistance. The coaches pulled the other way, arguing the "upside" of **individuality** and pointing out all the downsides of **consistency**.

AN INDIVIDUALITY POINT OF VIEW

- Acknowledges the reality that our population is "hard to serve" and requires case-by-case attention
- Able to care for people through a flexible and equitable approach
- Embraces each person's unique story and situation to foster a vibrant community

- Hard-to-serve people fall through the cracks
- Lose ability to care for people by becoming legalistic and rigid
- Lose the beauty that results from embracing everyone's unique story and situation

When the RSMs felt this surprising resistance, the immediate assumption they made was that they must not have been clear, that they must not have explained themselves correctly, because if the coaches understood them they obviously would have adopted their point of view. The RSMs once again would talk about how important **consistency** is and would tear apart an approach based on **individuality**—except that this time, they would be less diplomatic about it. Now they were convinced that the coaches would finally "get it," and would come over to their side.

But here's the thing: when we treat a polarity as if it was a problem and we have a tug-of-war conversation, *the clearer we are, the further and harder the other person (or people) will pull the other way.* This happens because in our attempt to be clear, we continue to say the same things over and over again, and the entire time we're talking the other person is thinking, *"He doesn't understand what I value, and he has no idea of the danger he is pulling us into."* The problem is that we are partly right *and* they are partly right, but because we are viewing the situation from an either/or, problem-solving perspective, we are both incomplete and vulnerable.

In the end, one side will probably win and one side will probably lose, but a few unfortunate things will result. First, a tug-of-war will never result in the best possible outcome. This polarized approach, with one side winning and one side losing, or each side giving up something and compromising, will result in an outcome that is far less than what it could have been.

Second, in our resolve and determination to win the tug-of-war, we will pull hard towards our side, even if means putting up with pain. If it is an actual tug-of-war, I will have a tendency to hold on so tight to my side of the rope that my hands will pay a price. In our lives and relationships, a tug-of-war conversation can result in relational pain, stress, and anxiety.

The final negative outcome is that the longer I stay in a tug-of-war and pull to win, the less and less I will focus on the higher purpose. Instead, I slowly but surely become solely concerned about just making sure that my "side" or "pole" wins.

Going back to my shelter example, as our coaches argued with our RSMs, the situation got further and further away from our shared higher purpose of FAIRNESS, and became more and more about which side was wrong and which side was right—**consistency** or **individuality**. The shared value of FAIRNESS was lost in the battle.

A Different Kind of Conversation

"The real purpose of searching after facts is not so we can manipulate the world to our advantage but so that our awareness can be transformed."

Peter Kingsley

So, how do I have a different kind of conversation and learn to speak the language of Polarity Management?

1. We have to start by recognizing that **there is wisdom in resistance.** When I'm dealing with a difficult conversation and attempting to get someone over to my side, yet find that they are pulling the other way, I need the humility to acknowledge that they probably see something that I'm missing. I need the discipline of trying to understand what they value from their point of view and what they fear about mine. I have to train myself to remember that resistance is not a bad thing that I need to fight against; instead, it can be an indicator of important wisdom that I otherwise may miss out on.

2. I also need to **value curiosity** in an uncompromising and ongoing way. If I realize during a conversation that I'm not truly curious about what the other person is suggesting, and that I'm closed to the reality that their ideas may contain wisdom and truth, that tells me I'm approaching the situation like a tug-of-war and only want my side to win. In his book *Seven Habits of Highly Effective People*, Stephen R. Covey wisely encourages us to "Seek first to understand and then to be understood." This means I need to *start* by trying to understand and embrace the point of view conflicting with mine. I need to find out why the other person is pulling that way. It doesn't mean that I have to give up—it only means that my goal is to fully understand the other perspective *first*. It also doesn't mean that I can't share my point of view. We are responsible to share the unique perspective that our bias brings; however, if we start with the goal of trying to understand the other side of the

picture, it often results in a greater opportunity to share our own, and to explore how two perspectives can work together to complete the whole picture.

3. We need to **ground the conversation in our shared higher purpose**. The longer we deal with a situation and the more intense or challenging the conversation becomes, the easier it is for the conversation to drift from the shared higher purpose and instead become a right-and-wrong battle of one pole versus the other. Don't lose sight of where both sides are aligned and have common ground.

   In our situation at the shelter, I knew that FAIRNESS was a non-negotiable value that *all* our staff believed in; we simply differed on what that looked like in practice. We needed to make sure that our conversation constantly came back to our shared value of FAIRNESS and didn't resort to simply debating **consistency** versus **individuality**. We have to keep the higher purpose as the foundation of our conversation—or we will simply end up in a tug-of-war.

4. The last value is the golden rule of this approach: try to *eliminate the word "BUT"* from your conversation. If someone is explaining why we should change the course of action and the first thing I say in response is *"Yes, but…"*, it means that halfway through their talking I stopped listening and started working on my response. When I start with the word *"but,"* there is absolutely no chance that I am trying to embrace their point of view. Sadly, I catch myself on this all the time. If I am passionate about my point of view I can get defensive, and although I'm trying to listen, my mind easily goes in a different direction. If I say, *"yes, but…"* it's a sign to me to slow down and stop the tug-of-war. With polarities, it is always right to say, "Yes, you have a legitimate point, *and* I think it is also true that…" We do not need to let go of our truth when we first acknowledge the other person's equally valid and essential truth.

Be Vulnerable

Often, being perfectly honest with someone about how you are feeling is the best way to speak the language of Polarity Management. Too often, we are hesitant to actually say out loud what is in our head, even though most of the time the other person is already aware of the emotions and energy we are giving off. Rather than pretending you don't feel the way you do, have the courage to say things like, "What you're saying actually makes me uncomfortable." In my shelter example, be vulnerable enough to say things like, "I have no idea how you feel like that approach is fair. To me that feels reckless. Help me see it". This level of candor and vulnerability can create a culture where everyone can actually say what they are thinking. It allows you to better understand the complexity of a situation and permits people with different viewpoints to be heard and understood.

When I talked to people about speaking the language of Polarity Management, I often had people push back and say, *"That's great for you, but you obviously don't know the kind of people I work with."*

That may be true, but here is what I have found: even if the other person is set on getting their own way, using these tips and values will still help you have a conversation that is much less of a tug-of-war. When you take the first step in initiating these tips, you will be amazed at how often the other person will respond in a way that is much more open and curious. When someone starts to understand that their point of view is truly being embraced, they are much more likely to be open and curious about your point of view as well. I believe that by nature most people don't always need to get their way, as long as they believe that their thoughts and values were truly heard and factored into the decision-making process.

Learning a new language is not an easy task—especially if we are trying to pick this up as an adult when we are set in our ways. This has been the case for me as I have been working on speaking the language of Polarity Management. I still make mistakes and fumble through it at times, and it still feels deliberate and not natural. However, it has been well worth the hard work. I find that I am able to have productive conversations with people to whom I used to struggle to relate. I also find that these conversations complement my natural way of thinking, and help me see things in a better and more complete way. This helps me make better, more informed decisions, and has resulted in a growing number of unexpected but deeply valued friends and allies.

To bring some closure to my previous shelter example, the woman was ultimately asked to leave and our staff was able to find a safe and suitable option for her in another facility. This is not the decision that I would have initially made; however, through information that came through a different kind of conversation, our team agreed that this was the most appropriate option—for her and our community. What also resulted from our commitment to a better conversation was the reality that there were more options for us to choose from than the two that we had originally been stuck arguing about—options that included having one of our coaches accompany her as she left, staying with her for the next day to ensure that she got the support she needed *and* to be absolutely sure that she made it to treatment. These win/win creative solutions rarely result from tug-of-war conversations, but become more and more common when we learn to speak a different language.

Personal Challenge: Learn the Language

Think of a difficult conversation you have had recently around your crux tension. Were you having a tug-of-war conversation, or were you speaking the language of Polarity Management? Think back to what you said, how you felt, and how the other person responded. Look at the following four steps and think about what you could possibly improve on if you were to have the conversation again.

1. Did you fight against resistance from the other person? Why?

2. In what ways were you (or weren't you) curious about the other person's point of view?

3. Did you have a shared higher purpose? What was it? In what ways did the conversation stay grounded in this higher purpose? In what ways did it become about defending your pole?

4. How often did you catch yourself saying "yes, but..." or preparing your argument while the other person was talking?

Step 4: Make Informed Decisions

IDENTIFY YOUR CRUX TENSION	**MIND YOUR BIAS**	**LEARN THE LANGUAGE**	**MAKE INFORMED DECISIONS**
Seeing is relieving	Embrace your opposite	There is wisdom in resistance	Go slow to go fast

"The key to good decision making is not knowledge. It is understanding. We are swimming in the former. We are desperately lacking in the latter."

Malcolm Gladwell

Have you ever been dealing with a really challenging problem only to have someone come along, size up the situation for about one minute, and offer what seems like an overly simplistic, clichéd answer? It can be an annoying, even insulting experience. I have seen this happen in our homeless shelter many times. Our team will be wrestling with a really tough situation and a volunteer who has been there for a shift or two will roll their eyes and offer what they see as an easy and obvious solution. But here's the thing: I have become more and more cautious of people who offer easy truths to complex situations. I don't fully trust clichés anymore. I am of the belief that when dealing with some of the big issues in our world—such as homelessness—simple answers just don't go far enough. If they did, no one would be living on the streets. It's not that there isn't some truth in these clichés; it's just that the truth is incomplete. In fact, I now believe that for every cliché that exists there is always an equally true but polar opposite cliché.

Let me give you a few examples. When it comes to the best way to get a job done, I am sure you have heard people say, *"If you want something done right, do it yourself."* That makes a lot of sense, right? But I bet you have also heard that, *"Two heads are better than one."* Two competing points of view, yet both are equally true.

GETTING THINGS DONE

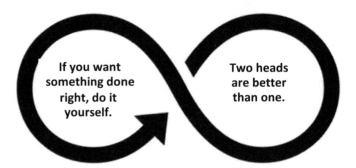

I have always been poor at team sports, but every coach I had as a kid would tell me, *"If at first you don't succeed, try and try again."* And I would try, and try, and try, until finally my eighth-grade coach had the wisdom and courage to look me in the eyes and say, *"Kid...don't beat a dead horse!"*

PERSISTANCE

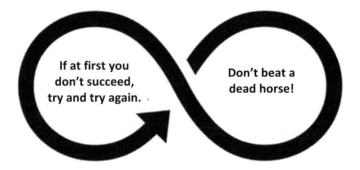

If you ever went to summer camp and had a crush on someone, you know that at the end of summer you and your sweetheart would take comfort in the fact that *"Absence makes the heart grow fonder."* And that worked well until about October, when you unexpectedly started to realize, *"Out of sight, out of mind"*.

LOVE

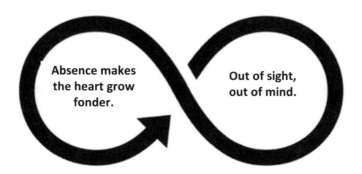

Early into his first term, Barack Obama was quoted in a Rolling Stone article saying, *"The issues that cross my desk are hard and complicated, and oftentimes involve the clash not of right and wrong, but of two rights. And you're having to balance and reconcile against competing values that are equally legitimate."* The guarantee of a polarity is that there will always be two *right* answers that are interdependent (one can't exist without the other over time). It is not just that I am right and the other person is also right, it is that my "right" and the other person's "right" are interdependent. *This means that my "right" is not helpful or sustainable without their "right."*

It's been my experience that the more responsibility we are given in life, the less often we find ourselves dealing with clear-cut problems to solve. Instead, we find ourselves wrestling with complicated issues, with a lot of complexities and competing values. I have found this to be true with the corporations I consult with and in the work I do with homelessness—and I expect that the same will be true for anyone who tackles the hard issues in life.

One of the biggest push-backs I get when I offer the concept of *healthy tension* to people is around decision making. People start to (falsely) believe that if they were to adopt this way of thinking, they would live in a world where everything would be equally okay, everyone would be right, and as a result, decision-making would be impossible. They tell me, *"This stuff is fine for you, but I live in a world where I have to make decisions every day; if I started thinking this way, nothing would get done!"*

This is a valid point, but I live in that world too. In fact, I don't think I could count the number of decisions I have to make in the homeless shelter each and every day. At the same time, I also have found that having the tool of healthy tension in my decision-making toolbox has resulted in better outcomes, allowing me to become a better leader.

Keep in mind something I said at the beginning of the book: healthy tension does not replace traditional problem solving. Many situations we face in life are straightforward problems to solve—things like policy and procedure, formulas and compliance, problems where there truly are right and wrong answers. There are other situations we face where we, like Barack Obama in the previous quote, deal with much more complexity, options that are equally *right*, outcomes that will significantly impact how well or poorly we leverage our crux tension. It is not that healthy tension stops us from making these decisions; we just want to be sure we have made the decisions in a polarity-informed way.

Go Slow to Go Fast

Of the hundreds of decisions that we make in a day, there are normally one or two that seem especially crucial. These are decisions that are directly linked to our crux tensions and will impact how well or poorly that tension will be managed in the future. As leaders, we normally have a sixth sense when we come across these situations, knowing in our gut that *this one matters*. And when we are faced with one of these significant decisions to make, it is worthwhile to "go slow to go fast."

Although putting our foot on the brakes when dealing with a challenging issue may slow things down in the short term, a good decision will most often allow us to gain momentum and work faster down the road. Furthermore, a polarity-informed decision will help us avoid unnecessary roadblocks and blowups later on—situations that could take ten times more time and energy to deal with in the future.

In slowing the situation down, you want to go back and make sure you have applied the steps we have already talked about:

- How is this situation connected to a crux tension?
- What is the higher purpose?
- How will the decision impact how well the tension will be managed in the future?
- What is your bias in the situation?
- What blind spots are being created by this bias? What might you be missing?
- Have you identified a teammate who would have the opposite bias, and have you tried to embrace their point of view in your decision-making process?
- What is at stake for you? How does this make you feel?

Sometimes this slowing-down process is only a matter of taking a few extra minutes, or making one quick phone call. Other times, we realize that we do not have to make every decision in the moment and that taking an extra hour, day, or even an extra week to gain the understanding and perspective needed will be well worth it down the road.

A number of years ago I took my own advice to go slow to go fast. When I look back now, I am so incredibly glad I did. I had been in my role as outreach director for a few years and things with local outreach were running quite well. As an organization, we were exploring how we could complement our local outreach strategy with a new global outreach program. To determine the best way to move forward, I spent close to a year meeting with focus groups from our community, engaging a group of strategic-minded business leaders to help advise me, and doing a ton of research and reading on the best ways to make a difference in the developing world.

About a year into this process, we confidently landed on an exciting idea and were preparing to pitch the plan to our community. It integrated the ideas and concerns that came from the focus groups, got strong buy-in from the advisory group, and was in line with what I understood to be solid international development practices.

A few weeks before we were about to "go live" with this idea, I got a phone call that had the potential to change everything. It was from a large global development agency, one we had learned a lot from and deeply admired. They had a solid international reputation for community transformation in some of the poorest and most desperate areas of the world—and they were calling because they wanted to partner with us. I was so honored. They had a new initiative in Africa that they wanted us to take the lead on. The only issue was that they needed to hear back from me right away due to the time sensitivity of the program they wanted us to run. Although it would be a total departure from the plan that I was about to pitch to our community, in my mind it was ten times better. I couldn't imagine saying no to such an unexpected and incredible opportunity.

In terms of the **stimulating innovation & change** vs. **preserving tradition & stability** polarity, I knew myself well enough to know that I had a strong bias toward **stimulating innovation & change,** so I thought that I had better be sure to thoroughly think this through before officially saying yes. And so I did, throughout the entire day and during the drive home. No matter which way I looked at the situation, it seemed like there was no reason in the world that would stop us from taking advantage of such an amazing opportunity. This was going to allow us to reach out to the poorest of the poor in ways we would have never imagined. I was so confident that I almost called them back that evening to sign on the dotted line. But I didn't. I decided that I would try to take my own advice and slow things down a little to make sure that we could go fast down the road. I decided to call a co-worker to get his take on the situation. Steve and I were very much aligned and excited about the vision and mission of our organization, but we normally saw the world through polar opposite points of view. He was the "yin" to my "yang." If anyone was able to see something that I might be missing—as impossible as that sounded to me—it would be Steve. So I sent him a text and told him I needed a half hour of his time the next morning. He responded and agreed to meet.

The next morning when we met, I spent the first five minutes explaining the opportunity I had been presented with and how I was planning to move forward. Then I told him that he had 25 minutes to show me what I might be missing.

And he did!

In fact, within minutes of hearing of the opportunity and my plans, Steve was able to point out factors that I somehow had been completely blind to. He showed me how this new opportunity didn't really acknowledge a lot of concerns and feedback offered in the focus groups. He noticed how it wasn't totally in line with the thoughts and guidance of my advisory group. He even challenged me on how it did not fit with some of the global development best practices that we had recently learned.

How could I have missed all of this? Within 10 minutes, Steve demonstrated to me that, in spite of my really trying to be objective on my own, my views were massively incomplete. I couldn't believe that in my excitement I had been so rash. I couldn't believe that I had almost let myself make such an ill-informed decision. It was incredibly humbling.

After taking some time to process Steve's advice, I decided to say no to the opportunity and move forward with our original idea. I am so glad that I did! Years later, I can see how this original plan has been a fantastic fit with the unique DNA of our community, allowing us to make a substantial long-term impact in some of the most impoverished communities in the developing world. It has exceeded all the expectations that we had. And it almost never happened. Had I not taken one extra day and decided to "go slow to go fast," we would have gone in a totally different direction; a direction that I can see now would not have been nearly as positive as where we are today.

Personal Challenge: Make Informed Decisions

Thinking about the month ahead, identify a decision you need to make that has the potential to significantly impact your crux tension. Now consider what it might look like if you planned to "go slow to go fast". Ask yourself the following questions about this decision:

- How is this decision connected to your crux tension?

- How will the decision impact how the tension will be managed in the future?

- What is your bias in the situation?

- What blind spots are created by this bias?

- Have you identified a teammate or partner who would have an opposite bias, and have you tried to embrace their perspective in your decision-making process?

SECTION THREE

The Road Ahead

A Better World ━━━━━━━━━━━━

You may remember that I started this book with a warning—explaining that once you start to grasp the concept of polarities and to pursue healthy tension, it changes everything. Tackling polarities and conflicting values is like trading in a recreational paddleboat for a white-water kayak. And although I say this with great excitement, I also know that it comes at a cost. And the cost is hard work.

However, the hard work is worth it! I have found that when our community is at its best, it is often at times when our crux tensions are put to the test and we are able to lean into them in a healthy way.

This was illustrated to me in a powerful way a few years ago. It was lunchtime at the homeless shelter, which is always one of the busiest times of the day. I was rushing around, helping out with food and checking in with some staff when a man I didn't recognize said, "Hello, Tim." I politely responded and continued to rush around with my tasks. I passed him a few minutes later and again he said, "Hello, Tim." I was not sure how he knew my name, but I acted as if I did and responded again with a friendly hello. Finally, a few minutes later when I was walking by, he reached out his hand to touch my arm to get my attention and said, "Tim, you don't recognize me, do you?" When he did this, I finally looked him in the eyes. My heart almost stopped. I was shocked because I realized that, in fact, I *did* know this man—it was John, a friend of mine I hadn't seen in close to a year. But so much had changed since we had last met. He looked as if he was about half his normal weight. And I could tell by the look in his eyes and the color of his skin that he was not well.

He went on to tell me in a matter-of-fact way that he did not have much longer to live—that the illness he was battling had finally won. He told me that he had nowhere else to go and that our shelter community was the closest thing he had to a home. He asked me if he would be able to stay with us in his final days so that he did not have to die on the streets.

This forced us to make a hard decision. Our shelter was not set up to be a hospice, but we could not imagine asking our friend to leave, so we decided to agree to John's request and allowed him to stay.

Over the next few weeks, our three crux tensions were put to the test in extreme ways. We knew that for us to live out our higher purpose of FAIRNESS, we needed to embrace both **consistency** and **individuality**, but John made this harder to live out than ever. We needed to maintain the structure and safety and being consistent, yet John was not able to sleep in our dorms, eat our food, and abide by some of our community rules.

We knew that for us to live out our higher purpose of being a HOME, we needed to embrace both **fun** and **seriousness**. The dire seriousness of John's situation was impossible to ignore and impacted the culture of our shelter, yet most days when I went into the common room at lunch, I would find John in his make-shift bed on the couch, surrounded by residents who were all crying with laughter. In spite of John's deteriorating health, his humor and sharp wit were healthier than ever and our community benefited greatly from it.

We knew that to live out our higher purpose of LOVE, we needed to embrace both **unconditional acceptance** (gentle love) and **accountability** (tough love). Having John stay with us, and seeing the way our community rallied around him (no questions asked), was a shining example of **unconditional acceptance**. At the same time, those of us who were close to John pushed him to place some tough phone calls and make amends with some people and situations he would have preferred to ignore. This even resulted in his daughter—someone who had been out of his life for decades—being able to come to the shelter and experience a side to her father she never knew existed. It was a life-altering experience.

Within two weeks of John staying with us, he passed away. I had the honor of standing beside him in the hospital room at the end, watching him leave a world that held a lot of pain for him and move into a new world where I believe he is experiencing perfect peace.

As I was driving home from the hospital, I thought of how proud I was of our community. I realized that this situation had pushed us to the limit. It was an exhausting, emotional, difficult experience for all of us. But I wouldn't have changed a thing. By making the courageous decision to live in tension and be okay with complexity, we had risen to a new level. We had moved closer to living out our vision and higher purposes than ever before.

Choosing to identify and embrace the key tensions in your life takes courage. It is the road less traveled and there are always easier routes. However, it is well worth it. Once you decide to take this path, you will never go back in a million years, or for a million dollars.

***

We live in an increasingly polarized world. My hope in writing this book is that it will equip and inspire you to embrace healthy tension; that you will acknowledge and accept that some situations in life are not problems to solve, but instead polarities to manage. And that by adopting a new approach, you will have the skill to conquer life's unsolvable problems, tapping into their energy to the benefit of your work and home—that you are able to courageously surf the waves of life with a confident spirit of adventure.

Godspeed!

May God bless you with discomfort at easy answers, half-truths, and superficial relationships, so that you may live deep within your heart.

May God bless you with anger at injustice, oppression, and exploitation of people, so that you may work for justice, freedom, and peace.

May God bless you with tears to shed for those who suffer from pain, rejection, starvation, and war, so that you may reach out your hand to comfort them and to turn their pain into joy.

And may God bless you with enough foolishness to believe that you can make a difference in this world, so that you can do what others claim cannot be done.

— Franciscan Benediction

Epilogue: Polarities and Faith

I was introduced to the phenomenon of Polarity Management and healthy tension as a business tool. I immediately realized that, although it was in fact a powerful business tool, it was so much more than that. This way of thinking has literally transformed my life and helped me to be a better leader, teammate, husband, father, and friend. Another area of my life that has been transformed through healthy tension has been my faith. As someone who was raised in a faith tradition where everything came down to absolute truth, clear-cut right and wrong, and good and evil, there was no room for complexity, mystery, and healthy tension. What I have been surprised to find is that although my faith is still one that embraces elements of absolute truth and either/or thinking, without blending this with the power of healthy tension and both/and thinking, my faith is both unhealthy and dangerous.

I could easily fill another book around the topic of polarities and faith alone. Knowing that this is beyond the objectives of this book, I will try to summarize my thoughts on polarities and faith through the words of someone much wiser than I. Years ago, someone sent me the following quote:

If we choose to live a more spiritual life, then we need to become more spontaneous, more engaged, and more contemplative. Living a spiritual life means we are able to live our life in total polarity.

This means we are at ease in the in-between spaces ...
Between traditional and progressive viewpoints
Between rational and emotional responses
Between taking action and just being there
Between solitude and leisure
Between fasting and feast
Between discipline and wildness.

If we are not growing in our spiritual life then we get stuck on one end of the spectrum or the other and we can end up bland, lukewarm, mediocre, and isolated. The only way to live a spiritual life is to be able to touch both sides at the same time. Knowing that it is in the interplay between living the spectrum (of these opposite polar forces) that we deepen our spirituality and become more aware of who we are, whom we choose to be, and in challenging times how we show up.

When I first read the quote, I found it incredibly convicting and powerful, but I was totally taken aback when I realized when it was written. This quote has been attributed to St. Teresa of Avila, a woman who was born in 1515. This was written 500 years ago! Seeing how the words are totally relevant to our world today, I am more convinced than ever that the concept of holding things in tension is not a fad or a trend. It is a phenomenon we need to understand and embrace if we are going to thrive at work, at home, and in our faith.

About the Author

Tim Arnold has spent over two decades helping organizations unite teams, spark change, and get unstuck. His clients include The United Nations, Citibank, KPMG, Toyota, and Siemens.

Tim is able to provide his clients with a real-world perspective through his experience launching successful for-profit and not-for-profit businesses, overseeing community outreach and healthcare programs, and managing international development partnerships in four continents.

Beyond leadership and team development, Tim is an avid outdoorsman, enjoys traveling, and is a really bad hockey player. His biggest accomplishments are being dad to Declan and Avryl, and husband to Becky.

Leadership Workshops
Team Training
Keynote Speaking

Visit our website and explore:

Public Workshops: A one-day workshop where leaders learn how to overcome chronic issues and conflicting values.

Private Workshops: A private workshop with learning outcomes that are tailored to your unique team and its workplace challenges.

Speaking: An enjoyable and relevant 1-hour keynote that will help you to unite your team, spark change, and get unstuck.

Want to see how well your organization is tapping into the power of healthy tension? Take the quiz:

www.thepowerofhealthytension.com/quiz

Visit: www.thepowerofhealthytension.com

Email: info@thepowerofhealthytension.com

Call: 289-723-2546

Additional Resources

Polarity Management
Identifying and Managing Unsolvable Problems
Barry Johnson, Ph.D.

Some complex problems simply do not have "solutions." The key to being an effective leader is being able to recognize and manage such problems. *Polarity Management* presents a unique model and set of principles that will challenge you to look at situations in new ways. Also included are exercises to strengthen your skills, and case studies to help you begin applying the model to your own unsolvable problems.

Polarity Partnerships
Organization and leadership effectiveness services and certification programs using the PACT™ Process, Polarity Map®, and the Polarity Assessment for more meaningful, measurable, and sustainable results. www.polaritypartnerships.com

Other Useful Resources:

Anderson, Kathy. *Polarity Coaching: Coaching People and Managing Polarities.*

Seidler, Margaret. *Power Surge: A Conduit for Enlightened Leadership.*

Wesorick, Bonnie. *Polarity Thinking in Healthcare: The Missing Logic to Achieve Transformation.*

All titles on this page are available at www.hrdpress.com, or through Amazon.

Acknowledgements

This book has been in the works for many years, and along the way so many special people have played a key role in getting me to the finish line.

Thanks to Christa who challenged me to get my butt in gear, and inspired me to believe that it was possible.

Thanks to Susan and Ally who had the patience and the skills to put words to so many of my random thoughts.

Thanks to Diego for taking the time to really "get it" and bring it to life through powerful images.

Thanks to Walter for challenging me to keep it simple.

Thanks to Bonnie, Chandra, Barry, Leslie, Phil, Tim, John, Fiona, Tim, Garry, Steve, Bill, Brian, Tom, Shannon, Greg, Mary, Nigel, Wendy, Mario, Mary, Dion, Jeff, Greg, Paddi, Vicky, Kelly, Kevin, Val, Sandra, and Cathy for taking the time to read through my drafts and provide such valuable insights, thoughts, and edits.

Thanks to Claudia for being a partner in this learning for almost 20 years.

Thanks to Joel, Ben, Jon, and Jeff for being an amazing inner circle, helping to keep me on track along the way.

Thanks to the Polarity Partnership community for your support for this project and your role in my life.

Thanks to the Southridge community for allowing me to experience and write about real life.

Thanks to Barry for your blessing, support, vision, and friendship.

And thank you to my incredible family—Becky, Declan, and Avryl—whose unconditional love and support continually overwhelm me.